THE SHAKESPEARE PLAYS

AS YOU LIKE IT

THE SHAKESPEARE PLAYS

AS YOU LIKE IT
HENRY VIII
JULIUS CAESAR
MEASURE FOR MEASURE
RICHARD II
ROMEO AND JULIET

THE
SHAKESPEARE
PLAYS

Literary Consultant: John Wilders

As You Like It

MAYFLOWER BOOKS
NEW YORK

Library of Congress Cataloging in Publication Data

Shakespeare, William, 1564–1616.
  As you like it.

  (His The BBC Shakespeare)
  I. Wilders, John. II. Title. III. Series: Shakespeare, William, 1564–1616. Selected works. 1978–
  PR2803.A23   1978   822.3'3   78–24133

ISBN 0-8317-0483-7

Manufactured in England

First American Edition

CONTENTS

PREFACE

Cedric Messina

Unisex and transvestite are words used very generally in the seventies, and *As You Like It* is one of the great statements of the style, although it was written at the turn of the seventeenth century. But when it was performed in the century of its writing, it had the added piquancy for the sophisticated theatre-goer that Rosalind, one of the great comedy roles of English dramatic literature, was always played by a boy – as in all Elizabethan theatrical presentations. So here was a boy playing a girl playing a boy! Ambiguities abound. Not even the great twentieth-century transvestite roles in the operas of Richard Strauss present so many variations of the male and female mirror. Octavian in *Der Rosenkavalier* comes nearest in duality – and then only in the purely comic scenes, and of course *he* is sung by *she* from the rise of the curtain. The transvestite roles of the Mozart operas are a special case. The most recent professional all-male performance of *As You Like It* was the National Theatre production by Clifford Williams at the Old Vic in 1967, in which Ronald Pickup was Rosalind and Charles Kay was Celia. Against all the odds of prejudice and prophetic doom, it became a tremendous success.

The role of Rosalind is much sought after by actresses, for apart from its comedy and warmth the role has one supreme inducement – its length. It is the longest role for a female character created by Shakespeare – 668 lines, only twenty-nine lines fewer than King Lear. The nearest in length to Rosalind is Cleopatra, who has 622 lines. Shakespeare's other great transvestite role, written almost immediately after Rosalind, is Viola in *Twelfth Night*, who has less than 500 lines to her credit. Considering the sexual mores of the Elizabethans it is puzzling how little Shakespeare made use of the device, but with both Viola and Rosalind he presented actresses with two magnificent opportunities.

The play has a long and distinguished history of performances at the Stratford-upon-Avon Memorial Theatre, and at the Old Vic Theatre in London, and many glittering names have been associated with the parts of Rosalind, Orlando and Jaques. It is Jaques who delivers the history of the 'Seven Ages of Man', one of Shakespeare's most quoted speeches. It is interesting to note that there is a fifteenth-century woodcut illustrating just that – the seven ages of man. The play has been filmed – notably in 1936 when the German actress Elizabeth Bergner essayed the Rosalind role and Laurence Olivier was her Orlando. The film was directed by Dr Paul Czinner. It has also been singularly successfully performed in the open air, notably at London's Regent's Park Open Air Theatre.

The Rosalind of this BBC Television production is one of Britain's greatest young classical actresses, Helen Mirren, one of the luminaries of the Royal Shakespeare Company. Indeed, whilst she was rehearsing for this *As You Like It* during the day, she was performing Queen Margaret in *Henry VI, Parts 1, 2 and 3* during the evenings at the Aldwych Theatre, where the trilogy was being presented by the Royal Shakespeare Company. *As You Like It* was first published in the First Folio of 1626, and it remains the only authoritative text for the play. The play has 2856 lines, of which 170 have been cut. It is twenty-first in the accepted chronological order of the plays, followed incidentally by *Twelfth Night*. This production was recorded in June 1978 on videotape by a light Outside Broadcast Recording Unit at Glamis Castle, Angus, Scotland, the ancestral home of HM Queen Elizabeth, The Queen Mother, by permission of the Earl of Strathmore and Kinghorne.

BBC Television is not inexperienced in the presentation of the plays of William Shakespeare, and indeed as early as 1937, on the first regular television service in the world, it presented a full-length version of *Julius Caesar*. Since then, thirty of the plays have been presented, the more popular ones many times over. Some have been produced in encapsulated form like *An Age of Kings*, some done on location like *Hamlet* at Elsinore with Christopher Plummer as the Prince and Robert Shaw as Claudius, and *Twelfth Night* at Castle Howard in Yorkshire with Janet Suzman leading the cast as Viola. Studio productions have included *The Tragedy of King Lear*, and *The Merchant of Venice* with Maggie Smith as a memorable Portia. Many productions have been taken from the theatre and translated into television terms like the Royal Shakespeare Company's *The Wars of the Roses* and the National Theatre Zeffirelli production of *Much Ado About Nothing*.

In the discharging of its many duties as a Public Broadcasting Service the BBC has presented during the last ten years, at peak

7

viewing time on BBC 1 on every fourth Sunday night, *Play of the Month*, a series of classical productions ranging from all the major plays of Chekhov to a number of Shavian masterpieces. Aeschylus has been produced in the series, and so have many of the plays of William Shakespeare. So not only in the presentation of Shakespeare, but also in the translation to the screen of the great dramatic statements of all ages and countries has the BBC demonstrated that it is fully equipped to meet the enormous challenge of *The BBC Television Shakespeare*.

The autumn of 1975 gave birth to the idea of recording the complete canon of the thirty-seven plays of the national playwright. (Thirty-six of the plays were published in the First Folio of 1623, exactly half of which had never been published before. The thirty-seventh is *Pericles, Prince of Tyre*, first published in the Quarto of 1609.) The first memo on the subject of televising all the plays emanated from my office on 3 November 1975, and was addressed to Alasdair Milne, then Director of Programmes, and now Managing Director, Television. We were asking for his blessing on the project. His reply was immediate and enthusiastic, as was that of the present Director-General, Ian Trethowan. This warm response to the idea stimulated us in the Plays Department to explore the possibility of making the plan a reality – six plays per year for six years, with one odd man out. It has been called the greatest project the BBC has ever undertaken.

There followed a succession of meetings, conferences, discussions and logistical quotations from engineers, designers, costume designers, make-up artists, financial advisers, educational authorities, university dons and musicians. The Literary Consultant, Dr John Wilders, was appointed, as was David Lloyd-Jones as Music Adviser. Alan Shallcross was made responsible for the preparation of the texts. On the island of Ischia, off the coast of Italy, Sir William Walton composed the opening fanfare for the title music for the series. Visits were made to the United States of America to finalise coproduction deals, decisions were taken about the length of the presentations to average about two and a half hours per play, and more seriously, the order of their transmission. This was a game played by many interested parties, some suggesting the plays be presented chronologically, which would have meant the series opening with the comparatively unknown *Henry VI Parts 1, 2 and 3*. This idea was hastily abandoned. A judicious mixture of comedy, tragedy and history seemed the best answer to the problem. It was decided that the English histories, from *Richard II* through all the *Henry IVs, V* and *VIs* to *Richard III* would be presented in chronological order, so that some day in the not too distant future the eight plays that form this sequence will be able to be seen in their historical order, a unique record of the chronicled history of that time. The plays that form the first sequence will be *Romeo and Juliet*, *Richard II*, *As You Like It*, *Julius Caesar*, *Measure for Measure* and *Henry VIII*.

The guiding principle behind *The BBC Television Shakespeare* is to make the plays, in permanent form, accessible to audiences throughout the world, and to bring to these many millions the sheer delight and excitement of seeing them in performance – in many cases for the first time. The plays were not only performed in theatres, for one of the earliest references to performances of plays by Shakespeare was made by William Keeting, a Naval Commander who kept a journal of a voyage to the East Indies in 1607. The entry for 5 September, off the coast of Sierra Leone, refers to a performance of *Hamlet*, and that of 30 September to a performance of *Richard II*, both being performed for Portuguese visitors aboard the East India Company's ship, *Dragon*. And so the plays started their triumphant progress of performances throughout the civilised world.

For students, these productions will offer a wonderful opportunity to study the plays performed by some of the greatest classical actors of our time. But it is a primary intention that the plays are offered as entertainment, to be made as vividly alive as it is possible for the production teams to make them. They are not intended to be museum-like examples of past productions. It is this new commitment, for six plays of Shakespeare per year for six years, that makes the project unique.

In the thirty-seven plays there are a thousand speaking parts, and they demand the most experienced of actors and the most excellent of directors to bring them to life. In the field of directors we are very fortunate, for many of the brilliant practitioners in this series of plays have had wide experience in the classics, both on television and in the theatre. The directors are responsible for the interpretations we shall see, but as the series progresses it will be fascinating to see how many of the actors take these magnificent parts and make them their own.

It was decided to publish the plays, using the Peter Alexander edition, the same text as used in the production of the plays, and one very widely used in the academic world. But these texts with their theatrical divisions into scenes and acts are supplemented with their television equivalents. In other words we are also publishing the television scripts on which the production was based. There are colour and black and white photographs of the production, a general introduction to the play by Dr John Wilders and an article by Henry Fenwick which includes interviews with the actors, directors, designers and costume designers, giving their reactions to the special problems their contributions encountered in the transfer of the plays to the screen. The volumes include a newly compiled glossary and a complete cast list of the performers, including the names of the technicians, costume designers and scenic designers responsible for the play.

INTRODUCTION TO
AS YOU LIKE IT

John Wilders

As You Like It is a comedy with practically no plot: it relies on its wit to keep it going. It was probably written in 1599, in the middle of Shakespeare's career as a dramatist, just before he embarked on the great tragedies. Seen in relation to his earlier works, it appears as the completion of a process whereby he gradually reduced the action of his comedies in order to concentrate more fully on the characters, their attitudes and relationships. Whereas the multiple plots of *The Comedy of Errors* (1592) and *A Midsummer Night's Dream* (1595) are intricately elaborate, the plot of *As You Like It* could almost be summarised on a postcard.

Such action as there is occupies the first act and the last six scenes, those parts of the play in which the malevolent characters, Oliver and Duke Frederick, either appear or make their influence felt. The events of the first act are primarily, though not entirely, a dramatic mechanism designed to propel Rosalind, Orlando and their companions into the forest; the concluding action provides a way of reconciling their differences and bringing them home again. This general movement of the play from the court to the country is one which Shakespeare also made use of in *A Midsummer Night's Dream*, *King Lear*, *Cymbeline* and *The Winter's Tale*, all of which are based on or derived from the popular works of fiction of Shakespeare's time known as romances. It was a form he used partly because it was ready to hand. In this play, such action as there is results from the tensions and animosities created at the court; the country is a place where people have the time and freedom from social responsibilities to talk, sing and engage in the leisurely pursuit of wooing.

The action portrayed in the first act is not, however, merely a dramatic device. It creates an impression of inbred and unnatural hatred which contrasts strongly with the hospitality and love shown in the forest. Moreover, because the court is associated with unnatural animosities, we are induced to feel that to live at court is itself unnatural and that the forest allows people to behave more nearly according to their natures. Although living conditions in Arden are far from comfortable, they are more congenial than at court: the winter wind is not so keen as man's ingratitude.

The predicaments of Orlando, a victim of a malevolent brother, and Rosalind, the victim of a ruthless uncle, are shown to be similar: he suffers the inhumanity of a brother; she of her father's brother. Moreover, the motives of Oliver and Duke Frederick are also alike: both are guilty of envy, the most inhumane of all impulses. Oliver is envious of Orlando because the latter is popular, 'of all sorts enchantingly beloved', so that Oliver is 'altogether misprised'. Duke Frederick turns against Rosalind because her very virtues, 'her silence and her patience', outshine those of his own daughter. Both villains resemble Iago, whose envy of Cassio is derived from the 'daily beauty in his life' which makes Iago seem ugly. Moreover, Shakespeare shows us not only the cruelty inflicted on the hero and heroine but also their reaction to it: they respond to this unnatural hatred by displaying its opposite, spontaneous and unselfish affection. Oliver and old Adam cling together in peril, and Celia and Touchstone take flight with Rosalind out of pure love and sympathy. They discover that the uses of adversity are sweet. Their positive response to their plight forms a link with the central acts where it becomes one of Shakespeare's major preoccupations.

As well as having practically no plot, As You Like It has practically no setting and in this, also, it appears as the end of a development. The wood in A Midsummer Night's Dream is richly particularised and, when the characters are inside it, they constantly remind us of its features, the 'bushes', 'briars', 'cowslips', 'acorns', 'wild thyme', 'woodbine', 'ivy' and 'eglantine' which make up the landscape. By comparison the Forest of Arden is characterised by its lack of features. It is seldom referred to in any detail, and the word used most frequently to describe it is a 'desert': the banished Duke calls it 'a desert city', and Orlando a 'desert inaccessible'. It is, simply, a deserted place. Whereas the vegetation of the Wood near Athens forms a kind of dark maze within which the characters become entangled and confused, the Forest of Arden is little more than an open space. This setting was ideal for the Elizabethan theatre, consisting as it did of an empty platform thrust into a group of spectators. Here again the absence of setting, like the absence of plot, leaves Shakespeare free to concentrate on the relationships between the characters. They respond to one another and not to the landscape. As a theatre historian has remarked, 'Shakespeare's is a drama of persons, not a drama of places'.

More significantly, the lack of setting enables each character to see in the forest whatever he is, temperamentally, inclined to see. It is not so much a place as a projection of the mind which enters it. Each character finds it 'as he likes it'. The idea that the landscape is neither more nor less than what you make of it is conveyed immediately on the arrival of Rosalind and her companions:

Rosalind. O Jupiter, how weary are my spirits!
Touchstone. I care not for my spirits, if my legs were not weary.

Rosalind. Well, this is the Forest of Arden.
Touchstone. Ay, now am I in Arden; the more fool I; when I was at home I was in a better place.

These snatches of dialogue obviously tell us more about the speakers than about the subject of their conversation. Similarly, there is a complete difference between the exiled courtiers' reaction to rural life and that of Jaques. The former express their feelings in a song of praise:

Come hither, come hither, come hither.
  Here shall he see
  No enemy
But winter and rough weather.

The latter shows his disgust in, appropriately, a parody of the same song. The predicaments of Jaques and his companions are identical but each adapts himself to it quite differently and thereby reveals more of himself than of his situation. One reaction is balanced against another and the audience is amused by recognising the discrepancy between the two.

The balancing and contrasting of one point of view with another is the way Shakespeare works in *As You Like It*. He offers us, instead of action, a series of arguments or debates. The little dialogue (III ii) between Corin and Touchstone is no more than an informal debate on the virtues of the courtly and the country life:

Corin. Sir, I am a true labourer; I earn that I eat, get that I wear; owe no man hate, envy no man's happiness; glad of other men's good, content with my harm; and the greatest of my pride is to see my ewes graze and my lambs suck.

Touchstone. That is another simple sin in you: to bring the ewes and the rams together, and to offer to get your living by the copulation of cattle; to be bawd to a bell-wether, and to betray a she-lamb to a crooked-pated, old, cuckoldy ram, out of all reasonable match. If thou beest not damn'd for this, the devil himself will have no shepherds.

Their argument is never resolved because each is judging the situation by his own standards. As Corin points out, 'those that are good manners at the court are as ridiculous in the country as the behaviour of the country is mockable at the court'. Your judgement depends on the attitude you adopt.

To write dialogue of this kind must have come easily to Shakespeare because, as a schoolboy at the grammar school at Stratford-on-Avon, he almost certainly followed the course of study common to all schools of this kind during the renaissance, which included instruction in the arts of rhetoric and logic and the practice of debate or 'disputation' where both skills were brought into use. In the schools and universities of Shakespeare's time, the students were expected not to write essays or carry out scientific experiments but to deliver arguments for and against propositions set for them by their teachers. Touchstone shows his skill in this kind of exercise when he replies to Corin's question, 'How like you this shepherd's life, Master Touchstone?' Here he adopts not a single point of view – for the defence or the opposition – but keeps changing his position from one to the other, sentence by sentence:

Truly, shepherd, in respect of itself, it is a good life; but in respect that it is a shepherd's life, it is nought. In respect that it is solitary, I like it very well; but in respect that it is private, it is a very vile life. Now in respect it is in the fields, it pleaseth me well; but in respect it is not in the court, it is tedious. As it is a spare life, look you, it fits my humour well; but as there is no more plenty in it, it goes much against my stomach.

He more or less demonstrates that the country – or, indeed, anywhere – is good or bad depending on how you care to look at it. As Hamlet says, 'There is nothing either good or bad, but thinking makes it so'. Or, in the words of Pirandello, 'Right you are if you think you are'.

Once the exiles have settled in the Forest of Arden, they turn their attention from their new surroundings to the business of courtship and love, and again Shakespeare constructs dialogue out of the clash between points of view. Orlando's feelings for

Rosalind are those of the ecstatic, idealistic lover and he expresses them in the exaggerated, figurative language of poetry:

> From the east to western Inde,
> No jewel is like Rosalinde.
> Her worth, being mounted on the wind,
> Through all the world bears Rosalinde.
> All the pictures fairest lin'd
> Are but black to Rosalinde.

Touchstone's view of her is much more practical and prosaic, and he shows his derision of the love-sick Orlando by giving a parody of his verses:

> If a hart do lack a hind,
> Let him seek out Rosalinde.
> If the cat will after kind,
> So be sure will Rosalinde.
> Winter garments must be lin'd,
> So must slender Rosalinde.

Both are obviously describing the same woman but their impressions of her could scarcely be more different. Each man sees in her his own idea of Rosalind. By this simple and entertaining means, Shakespeare reveals not only the character of each speaker but also gives us several sketches of the same woman. That is one reason why Rosalind seems to us a complex character.

The characters in *As You Like It* are divided, more or less, into idealists and realists. The former are imaginative, spiritual, inexperienced, impractical and tend to express themselves metaphorically; the latter are pragmatic, experienced, disillusioned and speak literally. In the courtship of Phebe by Silvius, she is the realist, he the idealist. To his complaint that he has been wounded by her eyes (a suffering endemic among renaissance love poets), she retorts derisively that eyes are incapable of inflicting wounds:

> 'Tis pretty, sure, and very probable,
> That eyes, that are the frail'st and softest things,
> Who shut their coward gates on atomies,
> Should be call'd tyrants, butchers, murderers!
> Now I do frown on thee with all my heart;
> And if mine eyes can wound, now let them kill thee.

She is, of course, correct, if we take Silvius's words literally, but nevertheless he is wounded if only metaphorically. Words change their meaning depending on whether you are in love or not. To Silvius, Phebe is an ideal woman to be served and adored patiently, but to Rosalind she is no more than an arrogant, heartless, plain-featured woman, one of 'nature's sale-work', and she tries to cure the doting lover of his illusions:

'Tis not her glass, but you, that flatters her;
And out of you she sees herself more proper
Than any of her lineaments can show her.

In Rosalind's opinion, the beauty of Phebe exists only as an idea in her lover's mind, in the eye of the beholder.

Whereas Silvius is blinded by love, Touchstone is a realist. He cares not for his spirits if his legs are not weary. He has no illusions about the 'foulness' of Audrey, but is content to put up with it because she is the only available means of satisfying his sexual appetites. She is 'a poor virgin', 'an ill-favour'd thing', but his own. Nor does he have any high expectations of his marriage: he does not propose to be faithful to her, nor does he think she will be faithful to him. But even though he assumes that Audrey will betray him, nevertheless he embraces marriage cheerfully if only because it is better than remaining single:

A man may, if he were of a fearful heart, stagger in this attempt; for here we have no temple but the wood, no assembly but horn beasts. But what though? Courage! . . . As a wall'd town is more worthier than a village, so is the forehead of a married man more honourable than the bare brow of a bachelor.

This readiness to venture on marriage with a full knowledge of its hazards is a positive attitude which he shares with Rosalind. As a woman disguised as a young man, she is at the same time as passionate as Silvius and as pragmatic as Touchstone. Privately, to her cousin Celia, she can confess 'how many fathom deep' she is in love; in diguise, to Orlando, she shows the other side of her personality and becomes the brisk, common-sense Ganymede, dispelling his illusions about Rosalind and love in general:

Rosalind.   Now tell me how long you would have her, after you have possess'd her.
Orlando.   For ever and a day.
Rosalind.   Say 'a day' without the 'ever'. No, no, Orlando; men are April when they woo, December when they wed; maids are May when they are maids, but the sky changes when they are wives.

She is the most subtle character in the play because she is intelligent enough to see everyone's point of view. She is also, like Touchstone, critical of herself and can mock the absurdity of her infatuation with Orlando even while she is possessed by it. She is ardent without being sentimental and inspires our confidence because she commits herself joyfully to love and marriage even though she recognises their risks. She enjoys her protracted courtship by Orlando – 'Come, woo me, woo me; for now I am in a holiday humour, and like enough to consent' – but at the same time she makes good use of her privileged position as Ganymede to try and cure her lover of his delusions: she wants him to marry her but in the same realistic spirit as her own. She wants theirs to be a 'marriage of true minds' in which her idea of Rosalind – as an unpredictable, fallible human being – will also be his.

It should by now be obvious that, although the dialogue in *As You Like It* is ostensibly about love and the country life, its implications are much broader. The idea that love is either ennobling or degrading depending on how you look at it can be extended to any experience, and indeed to human life in general. This partially accounts for the inclusion in the play of the one solitary figure, 'the melancholy Jaques'. Jaques is not a lover (he scoffs at the romantic Orlando) because he believes that love is an illusion, or rather that life is made up entirely of illusions. Whereas Touchstone, compared with the other characters, is a realist, Jaques is a cynic. His monologue on the seven ages of man is his manifesto. For him the world is a stage and man not merely an actor, but an actor in a drama which, from puking infancy to torpid senility, is futile. The lover's ardour is inspired merely by his mistress's eyebrow; the reputation for which the soldier strives is a mere 'bubble'; and man grows to maturity only to shrink back again into a second childishness, a regression to a more painfully ridiculous state than that from which he began.

That this is not Shakespeare's view of life is obvious from the eloquent arrival of old Adam at the end of Jaques' monologue; the old servant's loyalty, generosity and self-respect have no place in the cynic's conception of man. Moreover, Jaques is a prejudiced and unreliable moralist. He believes mankind is depraved because he himself has been a libertine and, as the Duke points out, attributes to others those vices of which he is himself guilty:

all th'embossed sores and headed evils
That thou with licence of free foot hast caught
Wouldst thou disgorge into the general world.

As Silvius's view of Phebe is distorted by love, so Jaques' judgement of man has been corrupted by debauchery. Moreover, the love which variously motivates the other characters is itself a challenge to his cynicism. Whether they are prompted by blind infatuation like Silvius, or physical need like Touchstone, or a combination of love and worldly wisdom like Rosalind, all the wooers act on the assumption that marriage is a worthwhile enterprise. Jaques, whose attitude is contrary to everyone else's, makes it clear that to him such an undertaking is absurd. By distributing these different points of view among the various characters, Shakespeare portrays the paradoxes and complexities of love, its delights, its pains and its absurdities. Only Rosalind is acute and sensitive enough, and has the openness of mind, to appreciate all these things. We therefore trust her judgement as she takes on the responsibility of resolving the confusions of the lovers and bringing the play to an end.

With the appearance of Hymen, the god of marriage, in the final scene, Shakespeare introduces yet another point of view:

> Then is there mirth in heaven,
> When earthly things made even
> Atone together.

The union of man and woman in marriage delights the gods because they recognise that, in it, limited human beings approach as nearly as they can to the perfect harmony of heaven. Hymen's vision of this multiple marriage may be genuine but it is not the whole truth, as we can see if we survey the assembled company. Silvius's view of his marriage to Phebe is not the same as her view of her marriage to him: whereas he has won the woman he adores, she has accepted a second-best to Ganymede who has mysteriously evaporated. Touchstone does not intend his marriage to last and, in seizing Audrey, he has thwarted the hopes of the unfortunate and dim-witted William. Moreover, though Hymen may celebrate matrimony as a 'blessed bond', Touchstone, as befits his character, sees it as a gathering of the 'country copulatives', and Jaques sourly compares the couples to the beasts embarking in Noah's ark. Though the characters are united in marriage, their points of view remain unreconciled to the very end of the play. And, although the Duke himself welcomes his sudden restoration to power, we ourselves, in view of his former contentment in exile, may see this fresh turn of events as fortunate or unfortunate, depending on how we care to look at it. Even when all the characters appear to have achieved more or less what they want, and we may tend to be cheered by the general spirit of reconciliation and fulfilment, Shakespeare adds an epilogue to remind us that the world we have seen is merely a stage and all the men and women merely players, and he invites us, through Rosalind, to like as much of his comedy as has pleased us. We find it as we like it.

Obviously this is a much more complex and sophisticated play than it seems to be, but its popular success in the theatre shows that it can be enjoyed by people who are unaware of its implications. It is a comedy of incongruities: the prospect of Touchstone, the courtier, accommodating himself with difficulty to the rural life and exercising his wit on the uncomprehending Audrey, of Orlando unwittingly professing his love to the woman he adores, and of Rosalind uninhibitedly confessing her feelings to her less than romantic cousin, are entertaining in themselves. Moreover, in spite of its slender plot, *As You Like It* is full of variety. There is a wide range of characters, each with a distinctive language and style, and they are brought together in various combinations: Touchstone with Rosalind and Celia, with Corin, with Audrey, with Jaques, with William; Rosalind with Celia, with Silvius and Phebe, with Orlando, with Jaques. Rapidly-moving, witty, colloquial dialogue is interspersed with long, formal speeches and songs. The audience's interest is constantly refreshed and revived. The predominant mood is confident and joyful, as the characters escape from the threats of their enemies, turn exile into a holiday, and gradually progress through courtship towards marriage. But although *As You Like It* is a romance, its effect is not merely romantic; it is unsentimental. The combination of a prevailing exuberance with a canny realism which distinguishes Rosalind is characteristic of the whole play. Shakespeare tactfully reminds us, largely through Rosalind, that, though men are April when they woo, they are December when they wed; that marriage, though a kind of ending, is also a beginning; and that life itself is but a flower in springtime. Perhaps Shakespeare's greatest achievement in this comedy is to recognise that life is a serious business but not to treat it too seriously. *As You Like It* has that quality which T. S. Eliot recognised in some seventeenth-century poetry, 'the alliance of levity with seriousness'.

THE PRODUCTION

Henry Fenwick

As You Like It was the catalyst that precipitated the plan to televise the whole canon of Shakespeare's plays for the BBC. The idea began when Cedric Messina was directing an outside broadcast production of Barrie's play *The Little Minister* at Glamis, where the castle was being used as a location. 'I went for the burn walk,' remembers Messina, 'and it seemed to me to be the most wonderful sort of forest. It occurred to me that if ever one were to do a location production of *As You Like It* then this was the place to do it. Working on *The Little Minister* had shown that there were many practical advantages for doing an outside broadcast there: there were no planes, no main road, plenty of co-operation from the village in providing food and working as extras.

'When I came back to London we considered doing it as a Play of the Month and we were discussing it when I said "Why don't we do them all!" So we postponed doing *As You Like It*, hoping against hope to get permission to do all the plays. So in a way it's been in preparation for years!

'I'd always felt that if you were going to do any of Shakespeare's plays as an OB then *As You Like It* is a natural. Ninety-five per cent of it takes place in the forest, there's not much of the castle, and Glamis is a very pretty, fairy-tale castle anyway, with a beautiful Italian garden: not at all the image of Glamis from *Macbeth*, you could never do *Macbeth* there!'

Shakespeare's plays, says Messina, are infinitely flexible: 'He knew they were going on tour – playing in halls, country houses, in the open air (in 1607 *Hamlet* was performed on a boat) – so the plays put up with a lot of pushing around. Why shouldn't they therefore be done on television, and as outside broadcasts? And *As You Like It* fitted completely beautifully into the bucolic setting.'

The apparently complex play, with its rather artificial plot, has consistently enchanted audiences. The story doesn't explain the appeal: two royal cousins run off to the forest to escape a usurping duke, the father of one. The other, daughter of the banished duke, disguises herself as a boy and while in disguise teases and flirts with the young man who is passionately in love with her. Lovers are paired, rights are wronged, love and marriage are celebrated in a final masque. What is the play's secret, I asked Messina.

'There's not much that's very serious in the play: the baddies all suddenly become goodies as though it had been done by waving a magic wand. The Forest of Arden, as Shakespeare describes it, is a fairyland: Camelot-land really. It's a comedy, I suppose, about sexual ambiguity. Everybody is slightly out of focus and it comes out very sexy!'

Director Basil Coleman had already worked on a Shakespearian OB with Messina when he directed *Love's Labours Lost* a couple of years earlier, and Messina also looks back fondly still on 'a masterly production of the opera *Billy Budd*'. The problems of OBs and of organising large and complex projects were not therefore likely to daunt Coleman. He feels, in fact, that he has been more successful with *As You Like It* than he was with *Love's Labours*. 'I've had that much more experience!' Some technological advances had helped too. 'The first time we'd taken a four-camera unit. This time it was a two-camera unit and they were much more mobile. They are lighter cameras and it is easier to position them. It meant that we didn't have to stage scenes to the cameras quite so much once we'd positioned them; instead we could take the cameras to the scenes.'

One of the hazards of going on location with a play, says Coleman, is the difficulty of making sure 'that the site doesn't take over. If you're going to go to somewhere like Glamis there's no point in going unless you use what it has to offer, but I had to make sure that we were never swamped by the surroundings.' Indeed, when making an outside broadcast drama, everything tends to begin from the location – designers, director, script editor, actors, all are affected by the choice of site. 'It's interesting exploring the location,' Coleman acknowledges, 'saying "All right, these are the places we *can* film, this is where the estate says we *may* film, where do I put this scene? Where that? What do I not have here that I want and need?" There were certain things the estate couldn't provide as completely happily as I had hoped: for example, the pastoral scenes on the edge of the forest which would include, I thought, fields for sheep and goats, the setting for the country characters – Audrey, Corin, Silvius where Rosalind and Celia – find a cottage to live in when Rosalind is banished from the court. Those settings were difficult to find on an estate. Perhaps that sort of meadow pasture scenery is more English than Scottish.

'We built a token cottage and had sheep pens, etc., and an unusual flock of sheep – don't ask me what kind, though I did know! But they are rather beautiful in their way, and a marvellous shepherd and his sheepdog came with them and kept them very very strictly. Sometimes indeed they wouldn't move when we wanted them to move. When Corin opened the gate of their pen I had rather hoped they would rush out and scare Touchstone [James Bolam], but would they budge? Not on your life! So we had someone at the other end, off camera, prodding them out till they did move, just enough, I hope, to be amusing, but not enough for people to think this is a Shakespearian play about sheep.

'It seems to me that *As You Like It* starts very much as a winter play, moving through spring into early summer. This we couldn't do – we were there shooting in early summer. What I tried, therefore, was: for the banished court scenes, to shoot them in carefully selected pine woods – selected, I might say, in late winter, early spring, when there were no leaves at all. I hadn't bargained for the fact that under these marvellous pine trees the ferns would grow three feet high! But they have such an extraordinary and unusual quality that I like to feel they have added something, even though they may have defeated my attempt to get a winter feeling.' He shrugs wryly.

'Other scenes were easier. Some we did in a very beautiful oak wood where bluebells were still flowering and the young bracken hadn't opened out and was still making those wonderful V shapes. It really hadn't been disturbed by people at all and for the love scenes this gave an untouched quality that I think was very effective. And we used beech woods for the final scenes where everybody is brought together. Mistakenly, *As You Like It* is often thought of as a pretty play, but it's not pretty at all. It's a very harsh play to begin with. I think the castle helped us there. I went indoors for several scenes: the banishment takes place in the crypt of the castle, which has a wonderful barrel-shaped stone ceiling, it's entirely this grey stone throughout. We took away a lot of the furniture to get back to the bare walls, which increased the feeling of medieval strength. Another small scene we played on a circular stone staircase. The outside of the castle I used for one or two scenes – for example, when the usurping Duke Frederick orders servants off to find the two girls. Also we used the Italian garden, which is a formal garden, for the first scene with the girls before the wrestling match. It's the only time we can convey the formality of the court. Then we did the wrestling scene 300 yards from the castle and built pavilions for Duke Frederick and his court, and an enclosure for the actual match, with the castle in the background.

'It was difficult to find the right site for the love scenes. They needed a certain seclusion without being too shut in. We found a marvellous chestnut tree of great age and beauty, with branches so heavy they bowed down to the earth and then grew upwards again. Under these huge sculpted arches of wood we staged the love scenes.'

In such circumstances I, as a layman, wondered what the set designer actually had to do. As tactfully as possible I asked Don Taylor whether his job wasn't extremely easy on location. 'On some OBs you never stop,' he says. Though he acknowledges that *As You Like It* was not as heavy as most. 'I can't move trees,' he points out with some satisfaction. The main task is that 'once the location is established you've got to make it work' and that can have unforeseen difficulties: 'Cows ate the first cottage we made.' And even without such acts of god or nature the designer's responsibility is onerous. 'You've got to organise a lot more – make sure that things you need come with you and come *on time*. Because once you're there you have no back up. But you get a good team effort on an OB. You've got to be sure you've got a lot of facilities around and craftsmen with you.'

With Taylor on the *As You Like It* location were two carpenters, two painters, a scene crew of about six, plus an assistant and a props buyer, building the ill-fated shepherd's cottage and its successor, the pavilions for the wrestling match, and working on the interiors. For one scene, in which Oliver, Orlando's unnatural brother, persuades the champion wrestler Charles to attempt to kill Orlando in the wrestling match, the director wanted a claustrophobic feeling which none of the existing interiors supplied. A room in the castle was therefore entirely panelled by the crew who were up there. 'You can only do that, though, with small things,' says Taylor. Normally what is there dictates, or heavily influences, the way things get done.

Luckily Don Taylor had worked with Messina on *The Little Minister* and so he already knew the location, which simplified his preparation somewhat. 'You've got to let the place speak for itself – the personality of the place takes over and its style determines the style both for sets and costumes. Working on location takes just as much research as studio work. You need masses of reference photographs to make sure that it all ties in. For example, in the wrestling match I needed to blind off certain bits of the castle. It was in the background and I had to hide its Victorian extension, so I made a medieval embroidered screen and used that in the foreground. And all the stands had to be positioned to make the sight lines of the cameras work conveniently. In the studio you can move the set about for the cameras – on OBs, once you've built something there it stays.

'The joy of a location is that you may start with a preconceived notion but then you find out once you're there that it won't work and that maybe anyway the alternative is better – or if it's not then it's up to you to use your expertise to make it better. It's a matter of planting my imagination into the area and making it work; and if you have to build something, make it look as though it has always been there. Looking for a place to put the cottage, you select the site that looks as though a cottage should be there and whack it in!'

Basil Coleman reiterates the point that the costume designer is 'every bit as much' affected by working on an OB. 'It's very difficult to design costumes to look acceptable against a natural background. It's something Robin [Fraser-Paye] manages very well – the clothes tie in marvellously with the brilliant greens.' 'Because it was an OB I was terrified of its looking like *It's A Knockout*,' says Fraser-Paye. The danger, he thinks, is in the all too vivid look which contrasting colours can take on against the green of the location. To avoid this he decided to go for grey/green rustic tones – Rosalind in pale leafy green, Orlando in bark colours: 'I wanted them to look as though they might all start climbing trees.' The castle again dictated the style: 'It's a very strong castle with a certain French romanticism about it,' Don Taylor describes. Consequently the clothes, says Fraser-Paye, have 'a vaguely medieval look about them – but it's not true at all, it's completely made up. It's like illustrations for a Victorian children's book, or for Lamb's *Tales from Shakespeare*. They're from a make-believe land. I tried to make the two central figures, Helen Mirren [Rosalind] and Brian Stirner [Orlando], look alike when she's dressed as a boy, so that for the first love scene they look like brother and sister. It gives the sexual aspect another perspective and I hope you forget all about the male and female.'

The overall feeling of the play, as Messina has pointed out, has a strong sexual tinge and this he didn't want to lose. With *As You Like It*, as with *Richard II*, the costumes of the men rely for their sex appeal on legs and codpieces – exactly the same emphasis,

Fraser-Paye points out, as today's emphasis on tight jeans. 'I tried very hard so that the clothes wouldn't get in the way of people's bodies. I feel very strongly that the sexuality of Shakespeare's characters is important and the designer should bring it out. Without the sexuality, in fact, I think you lose your play!'

I was surprised when not only the designers but even the script editor told me that his work was affected by the location. Very little in the play, says Alan Shallcross, needed to be cut and no scene was cut altogether. One or two obscurities were deleted but these were fewer than he had originally feared might be necessary: 'On the whole the vocabulary and language is very straightforward.' But slightly different pressures apply with an outside broadcast. 'The way you get from one scene to another is changed,' he explains. Because the scenes are to be fitted into a ready-made location, the leads in and out of scenes sometimes need to go. 'You often need to come later into the beginning of scenes – have slightly less scenery setting.' The main difference with an OB, however, is that it tends to spread rather more than a studio production. 'An OB tends to have more action: obviously you don't linger over entrances and exits for their own sake, simply because they look good, but in practice you can often make a dramatic, story-telling point by the way the view is used. For example, in an early scene between Orlando and the faithful servant Adam, Basil has Orlando's elder brother Oliver visible in the background practising sword-fighting while Orlando helps Adam at work in the garden. This makes a dramatic point and it's something you can never do in the studio – but you need to spend time letting it happen, making its point without any text. But in the process you lengthen the play and the script editor has to find a way to make up for that in some way and mustn't let the play become too long.'

Alan Shallcross had produced *The Little Minister* and was therefore another of the team who knew the location. So too did Helen Mirren, who starred in both productions. 'It felt like home from home,' she says; though this comfort didn't make the trials of outdoor shooting any less. The time lost because of natural hazards drives her crazy: 'In a twelve-hour day the camera, I think, must be actually rolling for about two hours and as a performer you have to do it that one time and get it right. The nice thing, though, was being able to see a playback on the monitor immediately. I enjoyed that – not because I could do it again if I didn't like it, but because it helped to see how to approach the next shot. And I enjoyed being outside – in fact I found it an invaluable help to be in a real forest, sitting on a real log.'

She had never been attracted to the play before performing it, she says, feeling (mistakenly) that she already knew it as a pretty pastoral play, well known from her school days. In fact she found when she began work that she hadn't known the play at all. 'It is much more complex than one thinks, and it becomes more and more difficult to penetrate. It has a pastoral romantic look about it and it's very easy to do it wrongly. It's a celebration of love, but of realistic love, not unrealistic love. It teaches you that you mustn't be misled by your early romantic feelings. But in fact it has a lot of different truths – it's a very hard play to pin down and that's what I came to love. You can say it's about this and it's about that, and it's not about any of those things – it has all those things in it.'

Coleman agrees with her: 'I personally think it's much more than an artificial pastoral. It's a very beautiful play, with so many things in it. It's an anti-materialistic play, if you like, about rediscovering Nature and our dependence on it. It tells us what nature can do to us, which is to cleanse, to purify, to teach us what we can do without, to help us learn gratitude. It touches on our responsibility to the environment, questions the need for courts and armies and self-protection. It rediscovers natural freedom. It touches more things than any other writing that I know.'

THE BBC TV CAST AND PRODUCTION TEAM

The cast for the BBC television production was as follows:

ROSALIND	Helen Mirren
ORLANDO	Brian Stirner
JAQUES	Richard Pasco
CELIA	Angharad Rees
TOUCHSTONE	James Bolam
OLIVER	Clive Francis
DUKE FREDERICK	Richard Easton
BANISHED DUKE	Tony Church
LE BEAU	John Quentin
SILVIUS	Maynard Williams
PHEBE	Victoria Plucknett
AUDREY	Marilyn Le Conte
AMIENS	Tom McDonnell
CORIN	David Lloyd Meredith
ADAM	Arthur Hewlett
WILLIAM	Jeffrey Holland
SIR OLIVER MARTEXT	Timothy Bateson
CHARLES	Dave Prowse
HYMEN	John Moulder-Brown
JAQUES DE BOYS	Paul Bentall
PALACE LORDS	Peter Tullo
	Mike Lewin
BANISHED DUKE'S LORDS	Carl Forgione
	Max Harvey
DENNIS	Chris Sullivan
PAGES	Paul Phoenix
	Barry Holden
MUSICIANS	London Pro Musica

PRODUCTION ASSISTANTS	Brian Morgan
	Terence Banks
PRODUCTION UNIT MANAGER	Fraser Lowden
CHOREOGRAPHER	Geraldine Stephenson
FIGHT ARRANGER	Terry Wright
VIDEO TAPE EDITOR	Ron Bowman
MUSIC COMPOSED AND	
CONDUCTED BY	Geoffrey Burgon
MAKE-UP ARTIST	Kezia de Winne
COSTUME DESIGNER	Robin Fraser-Paye
SOUND	Robin Luxford
LIGHTING	Clive Potter
MUSIC ADVISER	David Lloyd-Jones
LITERARY CONSULTANT	John Wilders
SCRIPT EDITOR	Alan Shallcross
DESIGNER	Don Taylor
PRODUCER	Cedric Messina
DIRECTOR	Basil Coleman

Produced on location at Glamis Castle, Angus, Scotland, between 30 May and 16 June 1978

THE TEXT

In order to help readers who might wish to use this text to follow the play on the screen the scene divisions and locations used in the television production and any cuts and rearrangements made are shown in the right-hand margins. The principles governing these annotations are as follows:

1. Where a new location (change of set) is used by the TV production this is shown as a new scene. The scenes are numbered consecutively, and each one is identified as exterior or interior, located by a brief description of the set or the location, and placed in its 'time' setting (e.g. Day, Night, Dawn). These procedures are those used in BBC Television camera scripts.

2. Where the original stage direction shows the entry of a character at the beginning of a scene, this has not been deleted (unless it causes confusion). This is in order to demonstrate which characters are in the scene, since in most cases the TV scene begins with the characters 'discovered' on the set.

3. Where the start of a TV scene does not coincide with the start of a scene in the printed text, the characters in that scene have been listed, *unless* the start of the scene coincides with a stage direction which indicates the entrance of all those characters.

4. Where the text has been cut in the TV production, the cuts are marked by vertical rules and by a note in the margin. If complete lines are cut these are shown as, e.g., Lines 27–38 omitted. If part of a line only is cut, or in cases of doubt (e.g. in prose passages), the first and last words of the cut are also given.

5. Occasionally, and only when it is thought necessary for comprehension of the action, a note of a character's moves has been inserted in the margin.

6. Where the action moves from one part of a set to another, no attempt has been made to show this as a succession of scenes.

ALAN SHALLCROSS

AS YOU LIKE IT

DRAMATIS PERSONÆ

DUKE, *living in exile.*
FREDERICK, *his brother, and usurper of his dominions.*
AMIENS, ⎱ *lords attending on the*
JAQUES, ⎰ *banished Duke.*
LE BEAU, *a courtier attending upon Frederick.*
CHARLES, *wrestler to Frederick.*
OLIVER, ⎫
JAQUES, ⎬ *sons of Sir Rowland*
ORLANDO, ⎭ *de Boys.*
ADAM, ⎱ *servants to Oliver.*
DENNIS, ⎰

TOUCHSTONE, *the court jester.*
SIR OLIVER MARTEXT, *a vicar.*
CORIN, ⎱ *shepherds.*
SILVIUS, ⎰
WILLIAM, *a country fellow, in love with Audrey.*
A person representing HYMEN.
ROSALIND, *daughter to the banished Duke.*
CELIA, *daughter to Frederick.*
PHEBE, *a shepherdess.*
AUDREY, *a country wench.*
LORDS, PAGES, FORESTERS, *and* ATTENDANTS.

THE SCENE : *Oliver's house ; Frederick's court ; and the Forest of Arden.*

ACT ONE.

SCENE I. *Orchard of Oliver's house.*

Enter ORLANDO *and* ADAM.

SCENE I
Exterior. Oliver's Orchard. Day.

ORL. As I remember, Adam, it was upon this fashion bequeathed me by will but poor a thousand crowns, and, as thou say'st, charged my brother, on his blessing, to breed me well ; and there begins my sadness. My brother Jaques he keeps at school, and report speaks goldenly of his profit. For my part, he keeps me rustically at home, or, to speak more properly, stays me here at home unkept ; for call you that keeping for a gentleman of my birth that differs not from the stalling of an ox ? His horses are bred better ; for, besides that they are fair with their feeding, they are taught their manage, and to that end riders dearly hir'd ; but I, his brother, gain nothing under him but growth ; for the which his animals on his dunghills are as much bound to him as I. Besides this nothing that he so plentifully gives me, the something that nature gave me his countenance seems to take from me. He lets me feed with his hinds, bars me the place of a brother, and as much as in him lies, mines my gentility with my education. This is it, Adam, that grieves me ; and the spirit of my father, which I think is within me, begins to mutiny against this servitude. I will no longer endure it, though yet I know no wise remedy how to avoid it. 22

Enter OLIVER.

ADAM. Yonder comes my master, your brother.

ORL. Go apart, Adam, and thou shalt hear how he will shake me up.   Line and stage
                                                    [ADAM *retires.*   direction omitted.

OLI. Now, sir! what make you here?

ORL. Nothing; I am not taught to make any thing.

OLI. What mar you then, sir?

ORL. Marry, sir, I am helping you to mar that which God made, a
    poor unworthy brother of yours, with idleness.   30

OLI. Marry, sir, be better employed, and be nought awhile.

ORL. Shall I keep your hogs, and eat husks with them? What
    prodigal portion have I spent that I should come to such penury?

OLI. Know you where you are, sir?

ORL. O, sir, very well: here in your orchard.

OLI. Know you before whom, sir?   38

ORL. Ay, better than him I am before knows me. I know you are
    my eldest brother; and in the gentle condition of blood, you
    should so know me. The courtesy of nations allows you my
    better in that you are the first-born; but the same tradition takes
    not away my blood, were there twenty brothers betwixt us. I
    have as much of my father in me as you, albeit I confess your
    coming before me is nearer to his reverence.   46

OLI. What, boy!   [*strikes him.*

ORL. Come, come, elder brother, you are too young in this.

OLI. Wilt thou lay hands on me, villain?

ORL. I am no villain; I am the youngest son of Sir Rowland de Boys.
    He was my father; and he is thrice a villain that says such a
    father begot villains. Wert thou not my brother, I would not
    take this hand from thy throat till this other had pull'd out thy
    tongue for saying so. Thou has rail'd on thyself.   56

ADAM. [*coming forward.*] Sweet masters, be patient; for your father's
    remembrance, be at accord.

OLI. Let me go, I say.

ORL. I will not, till I please; you shall hear me. My father charg'd
    you in his will to give me good education: you have train'd me
    like a peasant, obscuring and hiding from me all gentleman-like
    qualities. The spirit of my father grows strong in me, and I
    will no longer endure it; therefore allow me such exercises as
    may become a gentleman, or give me the poor allottery my
    father left me by testament; with that I will go buy my fortunes.

OLI. And what wilt thou do? Beg, when that is spent? Well, sir,
    get you in. I will not long be troubled with you; you shall have
    some part of your will. I pray you leave me.   70

ORL. I will no further offend you than becomes me for my good.

OLI. Get you with him, you old dog.

ADAM. Is 'old dog' my reward? Most true, I have lost my teeth
    in your service. God be with my old master! He would not
    have spoke such a word.   [*exeunt* ORLANDO *and* ADAM.

OLI. Is it even so? Begin you to grow upon me? I will physic   SCENE 2
    your rankness, and yet give no thousand crowns neither. Holla,   *Exterior. Oliver's*
    Dennis!   *House. Day.*
                                                                     OLIVER, DENNIS
                        Enter DENNIS.

DEN. Calls your worship?   80

OLI. Was not Charles, the Duke's wrestler, here to speak with me?

DEN. So please you, he is here at the door and importunes access
to you.

OLI. Call him in. [*exit Dennis.*] 'Twill be a good way; and to-
morrow the wrestling is.

Enter CHARLES.

CHA. Good morrow to your worship.

OLI. Good Monsieur Charles! What's the new news at the new
court ?   89

CHA. There's no news at the court, sir, but the old news ; that is,
the old Duke is banished by his younger brother the new Duke ;
and three or four loving lords have put themselves into voluntary
exile with him, whose lands and revenues enrich the new Duke ;
therefore he gives them good leave to wander.   95

OLI. Can you tell if Rosalind, the Duke's daughter, be banished with
her father ?

CHA. O, no ; for the Duke's daughter, her cousin, so loves her, being
ever from their cradles bred together, that she would have followed
her exile, or have died to stay behind her. She is at the court,
and no less beloved of her uncle than his own daughter ; and
never two ladies loved as they do.   103

OLI. Where will the old Duke live ?

CHA. They say he is already in the Forest of Arden, and a many
merry men with him ; and there they live like the old Robin
Hood of England. They say many young gentlemen flock to
him every day, and fleet the time carelessly, as they did in the
golden world.   109

OLI. What, you wrestle to-morrow before the new Duke ?

CHA. Marry, do I, sir ; and I came to acquaint you with a matter.
I am given, sir, secretly to understand that your younger brother,
Orlando, hath a disposition to come in disguis'd against me to
try a fall. To-morrow, sir, I wrestle for my credit ; and he that
escapes me without some broken limb shall acquit him well.
Your brother is but young and tender ; and, for your love, I
would be loath to foil him, as I must, for my own honour, if he
come in ; therefore, out of my love to you, I came hither to
acquaint you withal, that either you might stay him from his
intendment, or brook such disgrace well as he shall run into, in
that it is a thing of his own search and altogether against my will.

OLI. Charles, I thank thee for thy love to me, which thou shalt find
I will most kindly requite. I had myself notice of my brother's
purpose herein, and have by underhand means laboured to
dissuade him from it ; but he is resolute. I'll tell thee, Charles,
it is the stubbornest young fellow of France ; full of ambition,
an envious emulator of every man's good parts, a secret and
villainous contriver against me his natural brother. Therefore
use they discretion : I had as lief thou didst break his neck as
his finger. And thou wert best look to't ; for if thou dost him
any slight disgrace, or if he do not mightily grace himself on
thee, he will practise against thee by poison, entrap thee by some
treacherous device, and never leave thee till he hath ta'en thy
life by some indirect means or other ; for, I assure thee, and
almost with tears I speak it, there is not one so young and so
villainous this day living. I speak but brotherly of him ; but

SCENE 3
*Interior. Oliver's
Study. Day.*
OLIVER, CHARLES

'I'll tell thee . . . as
his finger' omitted.

'I speak but . . .'
to line 140 omitted.

should I anatomize him to thee as he is, I must blush and weep, | Lines 139–140
and thou must look pale and wonder.   140 | omitted.
CHA. I am heartily glad I came hither to you.   If he come to-morrow
I'll give him his payment.   If ever he go alone again, I'll never
wrestle for prize more.   And so, God keep your worship !   [exit.
OLI. Farewell, good Charles.   Now will I stir this gamester.   I hope
I shall see an end of him ; for my soul, yet I know not why,
hates nothing more than he.   Yet he's gentle ; never school'd
and yet learned ; full of noble device ; of all sorts enchantingly
beloved ; and, indeed, so much in the heart of the world, and
especially of my own people, who best know him, that I am
altogether misprised.   But it shall not be so long ; this wrestler
shall clear all.   Nothing remains but that I kindle the boy thither,
which now I'll go about.   [exit.

SCENE II.   *A lawn before the Duke's palace*   SCENE 4
                                                       Exterior. The Garden
Enter ROSALIND *and* CELIA.   *in the Duke's Palace.*
                                                       Day.
CEL. I pray thee, Rosalind, sweet my coz, be merry.
ROS. Dear Celia, I show more mirth than I am mistress of ; and
would you yet I were merrier ?   Unless you could teach me to
forget a banished father, you must not learn me how to remember
any extraordinary pleasure.   5
CEL. Herein I see thou lov'st me not with the full weight that I love
thee.   If my uncle, thy banished father, had banished thy uncle,
the Duke my father, so thou hadst been still with me, I could
have taught my love to take thy father for mine ; so wouldst
thou, if the truth of thy love to me were so righteously temper'd
as mine is to thee.   11
ROS. Well, I will forget the condition of my estate, to rejoice in yours.
C L. You know my father hath no child but I, nor none is like to
have ; and, truly, when he dies thou shalt be his heir ; for what
he hath taken away from thy father perforce, I will render thee
again in affection.   By mine honour, I will ; and when I break
that oath, let me turn monster ; therefore, my sweet Rose, my
dear Rose, be merry.   20
ROS. From henceforth I will, coz, and devise sports.   Let me see ;
what think you of falling in love ?
CEL. Marry, I prithee, do, to make sport withal ; but love no man
in good earnest, nor no further in sport neither than with safety
of a pure blush thou mayst in honour come off again.   26
ROS. What shall be our sport, then ?
CEL. Let us sit and mock the good housewife Fortune from her
wheel, that her gifts may henceforth be bestowed equally.
ROS. I would we could do so ; for her benefits are mightily mis-
placed ; and the bountiful blind woman doth most mistake in
her gifts to women.   33
CEL. 'Tis true ; for those that she makes fair she scarce makes honest ;
and those that she makes honest she makes very ill-favouredly.
ROS. Nay ; now thou goest from Fortune's office to Nature's :
Fortune reigns in gifts of the world, not in the lineaments of
Nature.   39
Enter TOUCHSTONE.

CEL. No ; when Nature hath made a fair creature, may she not by Fortune fall into the fire ? Though Nature hath given us wit to flout at Fortune, hath not Fortune sent in this fool to cut off the argument ? 43

ROS. Indeed, there is Fortune too hard for Nature, when Fortune makes Nature's natural the cutter-off of Nature's wit.

CEL. Peradventure this is not Fortune's work neither, but Nature's, who perceiveth our natural wits too dull to reason of such goddesses, and hath sent this natural for our whetstone ; for always the dullness of the fool is the whetstone of the wits. How now, wit ! Whither wander you ? 51

TOUCH. Mistress, you must come away to your father.

CEL. Were you made the messenger ?

TOUCH. No, by mine honour ; but I was bid to come for you. 55

ROS. Where learned you that oath, fool ?

TOUCH. Of a certain knight that swore by his honour they were good pancakes, and swore by his honour the mustard was naught. Now I'll stand to it, the pancakes were naught and the mustard was good, and yet was not the knight forsworn. 61

CEL. How prove you that, in the great heap of your knowledge ?

ROS. Ay, marry, now unmuzzle your wisdom.

TOUCH. Stand you both forth now : stroke your chins, and swear by your beards that I am a knave. 66

CEL. By our beards, if we had them, thou art.

TOUCH. By my knavery, if I had it, then I were. But if you swear by that that is not, you are not forsworn ; no more was this knight, swearing by his honour, for he never had any ; or if he had, he had sworn it away before ever he saw those pancakes or that mustard. 72

CEL. Prithee, who is't that thou mean'st ?

TOUCH. One that old Frederick, your father, loves.

CEL. My father's love is enough to honour him. Enough, speak no more of him ; you'll be whipt for taxation one of these days.

TOUCH. The more pity that fools may not speak wisely what wise men do foolishly. 79

CEL. By my troth, thou sayest true ; for since the little wit that fools have was silenced, the little foolery that wise men have makes a great show. Here comes Monsieur Le Beau.

Enter LE BEAU.

ROS. With his mouth full of news.

CEL. Which he will put on us as pigeons feed their young.

ROS. Then shall we be news-cramm'd. 86

CEL. All the better ; we shall be the more marketable. Bon jour, Monsieur Le Beau. What's the news ?

LE BEAU. Fair Princess, you have lost much good sport.

CEL. Sport ! of what colour ? 90

LE BEAU. What colour, madam ? How shall I answer you ?

ROS. As wit and fortune will.

TOUCH. Or as the Destinies decrees.

CEL. Well said ; that was laid on with a trowel.

TOUCH. Nay, if I keep not my rank— 95

ROS. Thou losest thy old smell.

Lines 40–50, to '. . . whetstone of the wits', omitted.

Lines 95–96 omitted.

LE BEAU. You amaze me, ladies. I would have told you of good
wrestling, which you have lost the sight of.
ROS. Yet tell us the manner of the wrestling.   99
LE BEAU. I will tell you the beginning, and, if it please your ladyships,
you may see the end ; for the best is yet to do ; and here, where | 'and here . . .
you are, they are coming to perform it. | perform it' omitted.
CEL. Well, the beginning that is dead and buried.
LE BEAU. There comes an old man and his three sons—
CEL. I could match this beginning with an old tale.   105
LE BEAU. Three proper young men, of excellent growth and presence.
ROS. With bills on their necks : ' Be it known unto all men by these | Lines 107–108
presents '— | omitted.
LE BEAU. The eldest of the three wrestled with Charles, the Duke's
wrestler ; which Charles in a moment threw him, and broke
three of his ribs, that there is little hope of life in him. So he
serv'd the second, and so the third. Yonder they lie ; the poor
old man, their father, making such pitiful dole over them that
all the beholders take his part with weeping.   116
ROS. Alas !
TOUCH. But what is the sport, monsieur, that the ladies have lost ?
LE BEAU. Why, this that I speak of.
TOUCH. Thus men may grow wiser every day. It is the first time
that ever I heard breaking of ribs was sport for ladies.
CEL. Or I, I promise thee.   124
ROS. But is there any else longs to see this broken music in his sides ?
Is there yet another dotes upon rib-breaking ? Shall we see this
wrestling, cousin ?   'You must . . .
LE BEAU. You must, if you stay here ; for here is the place appointed | wrestling, and'
for the wrestling, and they are ready to perform it.   130 | omitted.
CEL. Yonder, sure, they are coming. Let us now stay and see it. | Line 131 omitted.

Flourish. Enter DUKE FREDERICK, LORDS, ORLANDO, CHARLES, *and*   SCENE 5
ATTENDANTS.   *Exterior. Before the*
                                                                                           Duke's Palace. Day.
DUKE F. Come on ; since the youth will not be entreated, his own
peril on his forwardness.
ROS. Is yonder the man ?   135
LE BEAU. Even he, madam.
CEL. Alas, he is too young ; yet he looks successfully.
DUKE F. How now, daughter and cousin !
Are you crept hither to see the wrestling ?
ROS. Ay, my liege ; so please you give us leave.   140
DUKE F. You will take little delight in it, I can tell you, there is such
odds in the man. In pity of the challenger's youth I would fain
dissuade him, but he will not be entreated. Speak to him,
ladies ; see if you can move him.
CEL. Call him hither, good Monsieur Le Beau.   145
DUKE F. Do so ; I'll not be by.   [DUKE FREDERICK *goes apart.*
LE BEAU. Monsieur the Challenger, the Princess calls for you.
ORL. I attend them with all respect and duty.
ROS. Young man, have you challeng'd Charles the wrestler ?
ORL. No, fair Princess ; he is the general challenger. I come but
in, as others do, to try with him the strength of my youth.   154
CEL. Young gentleman, your spirits are too bold for your years.
You have seen cruel proof of this man's strength ; if you saw

35

Brian Stirner as Orlando and Arthur Hewlett as Adam

Orlando (Brian Stirner) wrestles with Charles (Dave Prowse). Le Beau (John Quentin) is on the extreme left in the background

yourself with your eyes, or knew yourself with your udgment,
the fear of your adventure would counsel you to a more equal
enterprise. We pray you, for your own sake, to embrace your
own safety and give over this attempt.   160

ROS. Do, young sir ; your reputation shall not therefore be misprised :
we will make it our suit to the Duke that the wrestling might
not go forward.   163

ORL. I beseech you punish me not with your hard thoughts, wherein
I confess me much guilty to deny so fair and excellent ladies
any thing. But let your fair eyes and gentle wishes go with me
to my trial ; wherein if I be foil'd there is but one sham'd that
was never gracious ; if kill'd, but one dead that is willing to be so.
I shall do my friends no wrong, for I have none to lament me ;
the world no injury, for in it I have nothing , only in the world
I fill up a place, which may be better supplied when I have made
it empty.   173

ROS. The little strength that I have, I would it were with you.

CEL. And mine to eke out hers.

ROS. Fare you well. Pray heaven I be deceiv'd in you !

CEL. Your heart's desires be with you !

CHA. Come, where is this young gallant that is so desirous to lie
with his mother earth ?   180

ORL. Ready, sir ; but his will hath in it a more modest working.

DUKE F. You shall try but one fall.

CHA. No, I warrant your Grace, you shall not entreat him to a second,
that have so mightily persuaded him from a first.   186

ORL. You mean to mock me after , you should not have mock'd me
before ; but come your ways.

ROS. Now, Hercules be thy speed, young man

CEL. I would I were invisible, to catch the strong fellow by the leg.
                                                      [*they wrestle.*

ROS. O excellent young man '

CEL. If I had a thunderbolt in mine eye,
I can tell who should down.   [CHARLES *is thrown. Shout.*

DUKE F. No more, no more.   195

ORL. Yes, I beseech your Grace ; I am not yet well breath'd.

DUKE F. How dost thou, Charles ?

LE BEAU. He cannot speak, my lord.

DUKE F. Bear him away. What is thy name, young man ?   200

ORL. Orlando, my liege ; the youngest son of Sir Rowland de Boys.

DUKE F. I would thou hadst been son to some man else.
The world esteem'd thy father honourable,
But I did find him still mine enemy.   205
Thou shouldst have better pleas'd me with this deed,
Hadst thou descended from another house.
But fare thee well ; thou art a gallant youth ;
I would thou hadst told me of another father.
                              [*exeunt* DUKE, TRAIN, *and* LE BEAU.

CEL. Were I my father, coz, would I do this ?   210

ORL. I am more proud to be Sir Rowland's son,
His youngest son—and would not change that calling
To be adopted heir to Frederick.

ROS. My father lov'd Sir Rowland as his soul,
And all the world was of my father's mind ;   215

Had I before known this young man his son,
I should have given him tears unto entreaties
Ere he should thus have ventur'd.
CEL.   Gentle cousin,
  Let us go thank him, and encourage him ;
  My father's rough and envious disposition   220
  Sticks me at heart. Sir, you have well deserv'd ;
  If you do keep your promises in love
  But justly as you have exceeded all promise,
  Your mistress shall be happy.
ROS.   Gentleman,
                    [*giving him a chain from her neck.*
  Wear this for me ; one out of suits with fortune,   225
  That could give more, but that her hand lacks means.
  Shall we go, coz ?
CEL. Ay. Fare you well, fair gentleman.
ORL. Can I not say ' I thank you ' ? My better parts
  Are all thrown down ; and that which here stands up
  Is but a quintain, a mere lifeless block.   230
ROS. He calls us back. My pride fell with my fortunes ;
  I'll ask him what he would. Did you call, sir ?
  Sir, you have wrestled well, and overthrown
  More than your enemies.
CEL.   Will you go, coz ?
ROS. Have with you. Fare you well. [*exeunt* ROSALIND *and* CELIA.
ORL. What passion hangs these weights upon my tongue ?   236
  I cannot speak to her, yet she urg'd conference.
  O poor Orlando, thou art overthrown !
  Or Charles or something weaker masters thee.

                    Re-enter LE BEAU.

LE BEAU. Good sir, I do in friendship counsel you   240
  To leave this place. Albeit you have deserv'd
  High commendation, true applause, and love,
  Yet such is now the Duke's condition
  That he misconstrues all that you have done.
  The Duke is humorous ; what he is, indeed,   245
  More suits you to conceive than I to speak of.
ORL. I thank you, sir ; and pray you tell me this :
  Which of the two was daughter of the Duke
  That here was at the wrestling ?
LE BEAU. Neither his daughter, if we judge by manners ;   250
  But yet, indeed, the smaller is his daughter ;
  The other is daughter to the banish'd Duke,
  And here detain'd by her usurping uncle,
  To keep his daughter company ; whose loves
  Are dearer than the natural bond of sisters.   255
  But I can tell you that of late this Duke
  Hath ta'en displeasure 'gainst his gentle niece,
  Grounded upon no other argument
  But that the people praise her for her virtues
  And pity her for her good father's sake ;   260
  And, on my life, his malice 'gainst the lady
  Will suddenly break forth. Sir, fare you well.

Hereafter, in a better world than this,
I shall desire more love and knowledge of you.
ORL. I rest much bounden to you ; fare you well.   [*exit* LE BEAU.
Thus must I from the smoke into the smother ;   266
From tyrant Duke unto a tyrant brother.
But heavenly Rosalind !   [*exit.*

SCENE III.   *The Duke's palace.*

Enter CELIA *and* ROSALIND.

CEL. Why, cousin ! why, Rosalind ! Cupid have mercy ! Not a
word ?
ROS. Not one to throw at a dog.
CEL. No, thy words are too precious to be cast away upon curs ;
throw some of them at me ; come, lame me with reasons.   6
ROS. Then there were two cousins laid up, when the one should be
lam'd with reasons and the other mad without any.
CEL. But is all this for your father ?
ROS. No, some of it is for my child's father. O, how full of briers
is this working-day world !
CEL. They are but burs, cousin, thrown upon thee in holiday foolery ;
if we walk not in the trodden paths, our very petticoats will catch
them.   15
ROS. I could shake them off my coat : these burs are in my heart.
CEL. Hem them away.
ROS. I would try, if I could cry ' hem ' and have him.
CEL. Come, come, wrestle with thy affections.   20
ROS. O, they take the part of a better wrestler than myself.
CEL. O, a good wish upon you ! You will try in time, in despite of
a fall. But, turning these jests out of service, let us talk in good
earnest. Is it possible, on such a sudden, you should fall into
so strong a liking with old Sir Rowland's youngest son ?   27
ROS. The Duke my father lov'd his father dearly.
CEL. Doth it therefore ensue that you should love his son dearly ?
By this kind of chase I should hate him, for my father hated his
father dearly ; yet I hate not Orlando.
ROS. No, faith, hate him not, for my sake.   32
CEL. Why should I not ? Doth he not deserve well ?

Enter DUKE FREDERICK, *with* LORDS.

ROS. Let me love him for that ; and do you love him because I do.
Look, here comes the Duke.   35
CEL. With his eyes full of anger.
DUKE F. Mistress, dispatch you with your safest haste,
And get you from our court.
ROS.   Me, uncle ?
DUKE F.   You, cousin.
Within these ten days if that thou beest found
So near our public court as twenty miles,   40
Thou diest for it.
ROS.   I do beseech your Grace,
Let me the knowledge of my fault bear with me.
If with myself I hold intelligence,
Or have acquaintance with mine own desires ;

SCENE 6
*Interior. A Hallway in
the Duke's Palace.
Day.*

Lines 35–36 omitted.

If that I do not dream, or be not frantic—   45
As I do trust I am not—then, dear uncle,
Never so much as in a thought unborn
Did I offend your Highness.
DUKE F.   Thus do all traitors ;
If their purgation did consist in words,
They are as innocent as grace itself.   50
Let it suffice thee that I trust thee not.
ROS. Yet your mistrust cannot make me a traitor.
Tell me whereon the likelihood depends.
DUKE F. Thou art thy father's daughter ; there's enough.
ROS. So was I when your Highness took his dukedom ;   55
So was I when your Highness banish'd him.
Treason is not inherited, my lord ;
Or, if we did derive it from our friends,
What's that to me ? My father was no traitor.
Then, good my liege, mistake me not so much   60
To think my poverty is treacherous.
CEL. Dear sovereign, hear me speak.
DUKE F. Ay, Celia ; we stay'd her for your sake,
Else had she with her father rang'd along.
CEL. I did not then entreat to have her stay ;   65
It was your pleasure, and your own remorse ;
I was too young that time to value her,
But now I know her. If she be a traitor,
Why so am I : we still have slept together,
Rose at an instant, learn'd, play'd, eat together ;   70
And wheresoe'er we went, like Juno's swans,
Still we went coupled and inseparable.
DUKE F. She is too subtle for thee ; and her smoothness,
Her very silence and her patience,
Speak to the people, and they pity her.
Thou art a fool. She robs thee of thy name ;   75
And thou wilt show more bright and seem more virtuous
When she is gone. Then open not thy lips.
Firm and irrevocable is my doom
Which I have pass'd upon her ; she is banish'd.   80
CEL. Pronounce that sentence, then, on me, my liege;
I cannot live out of her company.
DUKE F. You are a fool. You, niece, provide yourself.
If you outstay the time, upon mine honour,
And in the greatness of my word, you die.   85
                    [exeunt DUKE and LORDS.
CEL. O my poor Rosalind ! Whither wilt thou go ?
Wilt thou change fathers ? I will give thee mine.
I charge thee be not thou more griev'd than I am.
ROS. I have more cause.
CEL.   Thou hast not, cousin.
Prithee be cheerful. Know'st thou not the Duke   90
Hath banish'd me, his daughter ?
ROS.   That he hath not.
CEL. No, hath not ? Rosalind lacks, then, the love
Which teacheth thee that thou and I am one.
| Shall we be sund'red ? Shall we part, sweet girl ? | Lines 94–95 omitted.

| No ; let my father seek another heir.   95 | Lines 94–95 omitted.
Therefore devise with me how we may fly,
Whither to go, and what to bear with us ;
And do not seek to take your charge upon you,
To bear your griefs yourself, and leave me out ;
For, by this heaven, now at our sorrows pale,   100
Say what thou canst, I'll go along with thee.
ROS. Why, whither shall we go ?
CEL. To seek my uncle in the Forest of Arden.
ROS. Alas, what danger will it be to us,
Maids as we are, to travel forth so far !   105
Beauty provoketh thieves sooner than gold.
CEL. I'll put myself in poor and mean attire,
And with a kind of umber smirch my face ;
The like do you ; so shall we pass along,
And never stir assailants.
ROS.   Were it not better,   110
Because that I am more than common tall,
That I did suit me all points like a man ?
A gallant curtle-axe upon my thigh,
A boar spear in my hand ; and—in my heart
Lie there what hidden woman's fear there will—   115
We'll have a swashing and a martial outside,
As many other mannish cowards have
That do outface it with their semblances.
CEL. What shall I call thee when thou art a man ?
ROS. I'll have no worse a name than Jove's own page,   120
And therefore look you call me Ganymede.
But what will you be call'd ?
CEL. Something that hath a reference to my state :
No longer Celia, but Aliena.
ROS. But, cousin, what if we assay'd to steal   125
The clownish fool out of your father's court ?
Would he not be a comfort to our travel ?
CEL. He'll go along o'er the wide world with me ;
Leave me alone to woo him.   Let's away,
And get our jewels and our wealth together ;   130
Devise the fittest time and safest way
To hide us from pursuit that will be made
After my flight.   Now go we in content
To liberty, and not to banishment.   [*exeunt.*

ACT TWO.

SCENE I.   *The Forest of Arden.*

Enter DUKE SENIOR, AMIENS, *and two or three* LORDS, *like foresters.*
DUKE S. Now, my co-mates and brothers in exile,
Hath not old custom made this life more sweet
Than that of painted pomp ?   Are not these woods
More free from peril than the envious court ?
Here feel we not the penalty of Adam,   5
The seasons' difference ; as the icy fang
And churlish chiding of the winter's wind,
Which when it bites and blows upon my body,

SCENE 7
*Exterior. The Forest
of Arden. By a
River Bank. Day.*

41

Even till I shrink with cold, I smile and say
' This is no flattery ; these are counsellors   10
That feelingly persuade me what I am'.
Sweet are the uses of adversity ;
Which, like the toad, ugly and venomous,
Wears yet a precious jewel in his head ;
And this our life, exempt from public haunt,   15
Finds tongues in trees, books in the running brooks,
Sermons in stones, and good in everything.
I would not change it.
AMI.   Happy is your Grace,
That can translate the stubbornness of fortune
Into so quiet and so sweet a style.   20
DUKE S. Come, shall we go and kill us venison
And yet it irks me the poor dappled fools,
Being native burghers of this desert city,
Should, in their own confines, with forked heads
Have their round haunches gor'd.
I LORD.   Indeed, my lord,   25
The melancholy Jaques grieves at that ;
And, in that kind, swears you do more usurp
Than doth your brother that hath banish'd you.
To-day my Lord of Amiens and myself
Did steal behind him as he lay along   30
Under an oak whose antique root peeps out
Upon the brook that brawls along this wood !
To the which place a poor sequest'red stag,
That from the hunter's aim had ta'en a hurt,
Did come to languish ; and, indeed, my lord,   35
The wretched animal heav'd forth such groans
That their discharge did stretch his leathern coat
Almost to bursting ; and the big round tears
Cours'd one another down his innocent nose
In piteous chase ; and thus the hairy fool,   40
Much marked of the melancholy Jaques,
Stood on th' extremest verge of the swift brook,
Augmenting it with tears.
DUKE S.   But what said Jaques ?
Did he not moralize this spectacle ?
I LORD. O, yes, into a thousand similes.   45
First, for his weeping into the needless stream :
' Poor deer,' quoth he ' thou mak'st a testament
As worldlings do, giving thy sum of more
To that which had too much'.   Then, being there alone,
Left and abandoned of his velvet friends :   50
' 'Tis right ; ' quoth he ' thus misery doth part
The flux of company'.   Anon, a careless herd,
Full of the pasture, jumps along by him
And never stays to greet him.   ' Ay,' quoth Jaques
' Sweep on, you fat and greasy citizens ;   55
'Tis just the fashion.   Wherefore do you look
Upon that poor and broken bankrupt there ? '
Thus most invectively he pierceth through
The body of the country, city, court,

Yea, and of this our life ; swearing that we   60
Are mere usurpers, tyrants, and what's worse,
To fright the animals, and to kill them up
In their assign'd and native dwelling-place.
DUKE S. And did you leave him in this contemplation ?
2 LORD. We did, my lord, weeping and commenting   65
Upon the sobbing deer.
DUKE S.   Show me the place ;
I love to cope him in these sullen fits,
For then he's full of matter.
I LORD. I'll bring you to him straight.   [*exeunt.* | Line 69 omitted.

SCENE II. *The Duke's palace.*

Enter DUKE FREDERICK, *with* LORDS.

DUKE F. Can it be possible that no man saw them ?
It cannot be ; some villains of my court
Are of consent and sufferance in this.
I LORD. I cannot hear of any that did see her.
The ladies, her attendants of her chamber,   5
Saw her abed, and in the morning early
They found the bed untreasur'd of their mistress.
2 LORD. My lord, the roynish clown, at whom so oft
Your Grace was wont to laugh, is also missing.
Hisperia, the Princess' gentlewoman,   10
Confesses that she secretly o'erheard
Your daughter and her cousin much commend
The parts and graces of the wrestler
That did but lately foil the sinewy Charles ;
And she believes, wherever they are gone,   15
That youth is surely in their company.
DUKE F. Send to his brother ; fetch that gallant hither.
If he be absent, bring his brother to me ;
I'll make him find him.   Do this suddenly ;
And let not search and inquisition quail   20
To bring again these foolish runaways.   [*exeunt.*

SCENE III. *Before Oliver's house.*

Enter ORLANDO *and* ADAM, *meeting.*

ORL. Who's there ?
ADAM. What, my young master ? O my gentle master !
O my sweet master ! O you memory
Of old Sir Rowland ! Why, what make you here ?
Why are you virtuous ? Why do people love you ?   5
And wherefore are you gentle, strong, and valiant ?
Why would you be so fond to overcome
The bonny prizer of the humorous Duke ?
Your praise is come too swiftly home before you.
Know you not, master, to some kind of men   10
Their graces serve them but as enemies ?
No more do yours.   Your virtues, gentle master,
Are sanctified and holy traitors to you.
O, what a world is this, when what is comely
Envenoms him that bears it !   15

SCENE 8
*Exterior. Before the
Duke's Palace. Night.*

SCENE 9
*Exterior. The
Roadway leading to
Oliver's House.
Dawn.*

Lines 3–8 omitted.

ORL. Why, what's the matter ?
ADAM.   O unhappy youth !
　Come not within these doors ; within this roof
　The enemy of all your graces lives.
　Your brother—no, no brother ; yet the son—   20
　Yet not the son ; I will not call him son
　Of him I was about to call his father—
　Hath heard your praises ; and this night he means
　To burn the lodging where you use to lie,
　And you within it.　If he fail of that,
　He will have other means to cut you off ;   25
　I overheard him and his practices.
　This is no place ; this house is but a butchery ;
　Abhor it, fear it, do not enter it.
ORL. Why, whither, Adam, wouldst thou have me go ?
ADAM. No matter whither, so you come not here.   30
ORL. What, wouldst thou have me go and beg my food,
　Or with a base and boist'rous sword enforce
　A thievish living on the common road ?
　This I must do, or know not what to do ; | Lines 34–37 omitted.
　Yet this I will not do, do how I can.   35
　I rather will subject me to the malice
　Of a diverted blood and bloody brother.
ADAM. But do not so.　I have five hundred crowns,
　The thrifty hire I sav'd under your father,
　Which I did store to be my foster-nurse,   40
　When service should in my old limbs lie lame,
　And unregarded age in corners thrown.
　Take that, and He that doth the ravens feed,
　Yea, providently caters for the sparrow,
　Be comfort to my age !　Here is the gold ;   45
　All this I give you.　Let me be your servant ;
　Though I look old, yet I am strong and lusty ;
　For in my youth I never did apply | Lines 48–53 omitted.
　Hot and rebellious liquors in my blood,
　Nor did not with unbashful forehead woo   50
　The means of weakness and debility ;
　Therefore my age is as a lusty winter,
　Frosty, but kindly.　Let me go with you ;
　I'll do the service of a younger man
　In all your business and necessities.   55
ORL. O good old man, how well in thee appears
　The constant service of the antique world,
　When service sweat for duty, not for meed !
　Thou art not for the fashion of these times, | Lines 59–62 omitted.
　Where none will sweat but for promotion,   60
　And having that do choke their service up
　Even with the having ; it is not so with thee.
　But, poor old man, thou prun'st a rotten tree
　That cannot so much as a blossom yield
　In lieu of all thy pains and husbandry.   65
　But come thy ways, we'll go along together,
　And ere we have thy youthful wages spent | Lines 67–68 omitted.
　We'll light upon some settled low content.

ADAM. Master, go on ; and I will follow thee
  To the last gasp, with truth and loyalty.   70
  From seventeen years till now almost four-score
  Here lived I, but now live here no more.
  At seventeen years many their fortunes seek,
  But at fourscore it is too late a week ;
  Yet fortune cannot recompense me better   75
  Than to die well and not my master's debtor.   *[exeunt.*

SCENE IV. *The Forest of Arden.*

Enter ROSALIND *for* GANYMEDE, CELIA *for* ALIENA, *and* CLOWN *alias*
            TOUCHSTONE.

ROS. O Jupiter, how weary are my spirits !
TOUCH. I care not for my spirits, if my legs were not weary.
ROS. I could find in my heart to disgrace my man's apparel, and to
  cry like a woman ; but I must comfort the weaker vessel, as
  doublet and hose ought to show itself courageous to petticoat ;
  therefore, courage, good Aliena.
CEL. I pray you bear with me ; I cannot go no further.
TOUCH. For my part, I had rather bear with you than bear you ; yet
  I should bear no cross if I did bear you ; for I think you have
  no money in your purse.   11
ROS. Well, this is the Forest of Arden.
TOUCH. Ay, now am I in Arden ; the more fool I ; when I was at
  home I was in a better place ; but travellers must be content.

Enter CORIN *and* SILVIUS.

ROS. Ay, be so, good Touchstone. Look you, who comes here, a
  young man and an old in solemn talk.
COR. That is the way to make her scorn you still.
SIL. O Corin, that thou knew'st how I do love her !   20
COR. I partly guess ; for I have lov'd ere now.
SIL. No, Corin, being old, thou canst not guess,
  Though in thy youth thou wast as true a lover
  As ever sigh'd upon a midnight pillow.
  But if thy love were ever like to mine,   25
  As sure I think did never man love so,
  How many actions most ridiculous
  Hast thou been drawn to by thy fantasy ?
COR. Into a thousand that I have forgotten.
SIL. O, thou didst then never love so heartily !   30
  If thou rememb'rest not the slightest folly
  That ever love did make thee run into,
  Thou hast not lov'd ;
  Or if thou hast not sat as I do now,
  Wearing thy hearer in thy mistress' praise,   35
  Thou hast not lov'd ;
  Or if thou hast not broke from company
  Abruptly, as my passion now makes me,
  Thou hast not lov'd.
  O Phebe, Phebe, Phebe !   *[exit* SILVIUS.
ROS. Alas, poor shepherd ! searching of thy wound,   41
  I have by hard adventure found mine own.

SCENE 10
*Exterior. A Pine Wood
in the Forest of Arden.
Day.*

TOUCH. And I mine. I remember, when I was in love, I broke my
sword upon a stone, and bid him take that for coming a-night
to Jane Smile; and I remember the kissing of her batler, and
the cow's dugs that her pretty chopt hands had milk'd; and I
remember the wooing of a peascod instead of her; from whom
I took two cods, and giving her them again, said with weeping
tears 'Wear these for my sake'. We that are true lovers run
into strange capers; but as all is mortal in nature, so is all nature
in love mortal in folly.

ROS. Thou speak'st wiser than thou art ware of.

TOUCH. Nay, I shall ne'er be ware of mine own wit till I break my
shins against it.   55

ROS. Jove, Jove! this shepherd's passion
Is much upon my fashion.

TOUCH. And mine; but it grows something stale with me.

CEL. I pray you, one of you question yond man
If he for gold will give us any food;   60
I faint almost to death.

TOUCH. Holla, you clown!

ROS. Peace, fool; he's not thy kinsman.

COR. Who calls?

TOUCH. Your betters, sir.

COR.   Else are they very wretched.

ROS. Peace, I say. Good even to you, friend.

COR. And to you, gentle sir, and to you all.   65

ROS. I prithee, shepherd, if that love or gold
Can in this desert place buy entertainment,
Bring us where we may rest ourselves and feed.
Here's a young maid with travel much oppress'd,
And faints for succour.

COR.   Fair sir, I pity her,   70
And wish, for her sake more than for mine own,
My fortunes were more able to relieve her;
But I am shepherd to another man,
And do not shear the fleeces that I graze.
My master is of churlish disposition,   75
And little recks to find the way to heaven
By doing deeds of hospitality.
Besides, his cote, his flocks, and bounds of feed,
Are now on sale; and at our sheepcote now,
By reason of his absence, there is nothing   80
That you will feed on; but what is, come see,
And in my voice most welcome shall you be.

ROS. What is he that shall buy his flock and pasture?

COR. That young swain that you saw here but erewhile,
That little cares for buying any thing.   85

ROS. I pray thee, if it stand with honesty,
Buy thou the cottage, pasture, and the flock,
And thou shalt have to pay for it of us.

CEL. And we will mend thy wages. I like this place,
And willingly could waste my time in it.   90

COR. Assuredly the thing is to be sold.
Go with me; if you like upon report
The soil, the profit, and this kind of life,

I will your very faithful feeder be,
And buy it with your gold right suddenly.   [*exeunt.*

SCENE V. *Another part of the Forest.*

Enter AMIENS, JAQUES, *and* OTHERS.

Song.

SCENE 11
*Exterior. A Grove of
Yew Trees in the
Forest of Arden. Day.*

AMI.   Under the greenwood tree
              Who loves to lie with me,
              And turn his merry note
              Unto the sweet bird's throat,
          Come hither, come hither, come hither.   5
              Here shall he see
              No enemy
          But winter and rough weather.

JAQ. More, more, I prithee, more.
AMI. It will make you melancholy, Monsieur Jaques.
JAQ. I thank it. More, I prithee, more. I can suck melancholy out
    of a song, as a weasel sucks eggs. More, I prithee, more. 13
AMI. My voice is ragged ; I know I cannot please you.
JAQ. I do not desire you to please me ; I do desire you to sing.
    Come, more ; another stanzo. Call you 'em stanzos ?
AMI. What you will, Monsieur Jaques.
JAQ. Nay, I care not for their names ; they owe me nothing. Will
    you sing ?
AMI. More at your request than to please myself.   20
JAQ. Well then, if ever I thank any man, I'll thank you ; but that
    they call compliment is like th' encounter of two dog-apes ; and
    when a man thanks me heartily, methinks I have given him a
    penny, and he renders me the beggarly thanks. Come, sing ;
    and you that will not, hold your tongues.   26
AMI. Well, I'll end the song. Sirs, cover the while ; the Duke will
    drink under this tree. He hath been all this day to look you.
JAQ. And I have been all this day to avoid him. He is too disputable
    for my company. I think of as many matters as he ; but I give
    heaven thanks, and make no boast of them. Come, warble, come.

'But that . . .
beggarly thanks'
omitted.

Song.

All together here.

          Who doth ambition shun,
          And loves to live i' th' sun,
          Seeking the food he eats,
          And pleas'd with what he gets,   35
      Come hither, come hither, come hither.
          Here shall he see
          No enemy
      But winter and rough weather.   40

JAQ. I'll give you a verse to this note that I made yesterday in despite
    of my invention.
AMI. And I'll sing it.

47

JAQ. Thus it goes :   45
    If it do come to pass
    That any man turn ass,
    Leaving his wealth and ease
    A stubborn will to please,
    Ducdame, ducdame, ducdame ;   50
    Here shall he see
    Gross fools as he,
    An if he will come to me.
AMI. What's that ' ducdame ' ?
JAQ. 'Tis a Greek invocation, to call fools into a circle.   I'll go sleep,
    if I can ; if I cannot, I'll rail against all the first-born of Egypt.
| AMI. And I'll go seek the Duke ; his banquet is prepar'd.   59 | Line 59 omitted.
                                          [exeunt severally. AMIENS sings 'If it do
come to pass . . .'

SCENE VI.   *The forest.*   SCENE 12
Exterior. A Pine Wood
Enter ORLANDO *and* ADAM.   *in the Forest of Arden.*
Dusk.

ADAM. Dear master, I can go no further.   O, I die for food !   Here
    lie I down, and measure out my grave.   Farewell, kind master.
ORL. Why, how now, Adam !   No greater heart in thee ?   Live a
    little ;   comfort a little ;   cheer thyself a little.   If this uncouth
    forest yield anything savage, I will either be food for it or bring
    it for food to thee.   Thy conceit is nearer death than thy powers.
    For my sake be comfortable ;   hold death awhile at the arm's
    end.   I will here be with thee presently ;   and if I bring thee
    not something to eat, I will give thee leave to die ;   but if thou
    diest before I come, thou art a mocker of my labour.   Well said !
    thou look'st cheerly ;   and I'll be with thee quickly.   Yet thou
    liest in the bleak air.   Come, I will bear thee to some shelter ;
    and thou shalt not die for lack of a dinner, if there live any thing
    in this desert.   Cheerly, good Adam !   *[exeunt.*

SCENE VII.   *The forest.*   SCENE 13
Exterior. A Grove of
A table set out.   Enter DUKE SENIOR, AMIENS, *and* LORDS, *like outlaws.*   *Yew Trees in the*
Forest of Arden.
DUKE S. I think he be transform'd into a beast ;   *Night.*
    For I can nowhere find him like a man.   DUKE SENIOR,
I LORD. My lord, he is but even now gone hence ;   JAQUES, AMIENS, and
    Here was he merry, hearing of a song.   LORDS
DUKE S. If he, compact of jars, grow musical,   5
    We shall have shortly discord in the spheres.   Lines 7–8 and stage
    Go seek him ;   tell him I would speak with him.   direction omitted.

Enter JAQUES.

I LORD. He saves my labour by his own approach.
DUKE S. Why, how now, monsieur !   what a life is this,
    That your poor friends must woo your company ?   10
    What, you look merrily !
JAQ. A fool, a fool !   I met a fool i' th' forest,
    A motley fool.   A miserable world !
    As I do live by food, I met a fool,
    Who laid him down and bask'd him in the sun,   15

Brian Stirner as Orlando

Helen Mirren as Rosalind

Angharad Rees as Celia

Duke Frederick (Richard Easton, centre) at the wrestling with Celia (Angharad Rees) and Rosalind (Helen Mirren)

James Bolam as Touchstone and Marilyn Le Conte as Audrey

From left to right: Orlando (Brian Stirner), Jaques (Richard Pasco), lords and (foreground right) the Banished Duke (Tony Church)

Hymen (John Moulder-Brown) with Celia (left) and Rosalind

Victoria Plucknett as Phebe

Maynard Williams as Silvius and David Lloyd Meredith as Corin

Clive Francis as Oliver

Richard Pasco as Jaques

And rail'd on Lady Fortune in good terms,
In good set terms—and yet a motley fool.
' Good morrow, fool ' quoth I ; ' No, sir,' quoth he
  ' Call me not fool till heaven hath sent me fortune.'
And then he drew a dial from his poke,   20
And, looking on it with lack-lustre eye,
Says very wisely ' It is ten o'clock ;
Thus we may see ' quoth he ' how the world wags ;
'Tis but an hour ago since it was nine ;
And after one hour more 'twill be eleven ;   25
And so, from hour to hour, we ripe and ripe,
And then, from hour to hour, we rot and rot ;
And thereby hangs a tale'.   When I did hear
The motley fool thus moral on the time,
My lungs began to crow like chanticleer   30
That fools should be so deep contemplative ;
And I did laugh sans intermission
An hour by his dial.   O noble fool !
A worthy fool !   Motley's the only wear.
DUKE S. What fool is this ?   35
JAQ. O worthy fool !   One that hath been a courtier,
And says, if ladies be but young and fair,
They have the gift to know it ; and in his brain,
Which is as dry as the remainder biscuit
After a voyage, he hath strange places cramm'd   40
With observation, the which he vents
In mangled forms.   O that I were a fool !
I am ambitious for a motley coat.
DUKE S. Thou shalt have one.
JAQ.   It is my only suit,
Provided that you weed your better judgments   45
Of all opinion that grows rank in them
That I am wise.   I must have liberty
Withal, as large a charter as the wind,
To blow on whom I please, for so fools have ;
And they that are most galled with my folly,   50 | Lines 50–57 omitted.
They most must laugh.   And why, sir, must they so ?
The why is plain as way to parish church :
He that a fool doth very wisely hit
Doth very foolishly, although he smart,
Not to seem senseless of the bob ; if not,   55
The wise man's folly is anatomiz'd
Even by the squand'ring glances of the fool.
Invest me in my motley ; give me leave
To speak my mind, and I will through and through
Cleanse the foul body of th' infected world,   60
If they will patiently receive my medicine.
DUKE S. Fie on thee !   I can tell what thou wouldst do.
JAQ. What, for a counter, would I do but good ?
DUKE S. Most mischievous foul sin, in chiding sin ;
For thou thyself hast been a libertine,   65
As sensual as the brutish sting itself ;
And all th' embossed sores and headed evils
That thou with license of free foot hast caught

Wouldst thou disgorge into the general world.
JAQ. Why, who cries out on pride   70
  That can therein tax any private party?
  Doth it not flow as hugely as the sea,
  Till that the wearer's very means do ebb?
  What woman in the city do I name
  When that I say the city-woman bears   75
  The cost of princes on unworthy shoulders?
  Who can come in and say that I mean her,
  When such a one as she such is her neighbour?   ORLANDO *enters here,*
  Or what is he of basest function   *with sword drawn.*
  That says his bravery is not on my cost,   80
  Thinking that I mean him, but therein suits
  His folly to the mettle of my speech?
  There then! how then? what then? Let me see wherein
  My tongue hath wrong'd him : if it do him right,
  Then he hath wrong'd himself ; if he be free,   85
  Why then my taxing like a wild-goose flies,
  Unclaim'd of any man.   But who comes here?

     Enter ORLANDO, *with his sword drawn.*   See above.

ORL. Forbear, and eat no more.
JAQ.   Why, I have eat none yet.
ORL. Nor shalt not, till necessity be serv'd.
JAQ. Of what kind should this cock come of?   90
DUKE S. Art thou thus bolden'd, man by thy distress?
  Or else a rude despiser of good manners,
  That in civility thou seem'st so empty?
ORL. You touch'd my vein at first : the thorny point
  Of bare distress hath ta'en from me the show   95
  Of smooth civility ; yet am I inland bred,
  And know some nurture.   But forbear, I say ;
  He dies that touches any of this fruit
  Till I and my affairs are answered.
JAQ. An you will not be answer'd with reason, I must die.
DUKE S. What would you have?   Your gentleness shall force
  More than your force move us to gentleness.
ORL. I almost die for food, and let me have it.
DUKE S. Sit down and feed, and welcome to our table.   105
ORL. Speak you so gently?   Pardon me, I pray you ;
  I thought that all things had been savage here,
  And therefore put I on the countenance
  Of stern commandment.   But whate'er you are
  That in this desert inaccessible,   110
  Under the shade of melancholy boughs,
  Lose and neglect the creeping hours of time ;
  If ever you have look'd on better days,
  If ever been where bells have knoll'd to church,
  If ever sat at any good man's feast,   115
  If ever from your eyelids wip'd a tear,
  And know what 'tis to pity and be pitied,
  Let gentleness my strong enforcement be ;
  In the which hope I blush, and hide my sword.

DUKE S. True is it that we have seen better days,　　　120
And have with holy bell been knoll'd to church,
And sat at good men's feasts, and wip'd our eyes
Of drops that sacred pity hath engend'red ;
And therefore sit you down in gentleness,
And take upon command what help we have　　　125
That to your wanting may be minist'red.
ORL. Then but forbear your food a little while,
Whiles, like a doe, I go to find my fawn,
And give it food. There is an old poor man
Who after me hath many a weary step　　　130
Limp'd in pure love ; till he be first suffic'd,
Oppress'd with two weak evils, age and hunger,
I will not touch a bit.
DUKE S.　　　　　　　Go find him out.
And we will nothing waste till you return.
ORL. I thank ye ; and be blest for your good comfort !　　[*exit.*
DUKE S. Thou seest we are not all alone unhappy :　　　136
This wide and universal theatre
Presents more woeful pageants than the scene
Wherein we play in.
JAQ.　　　　　　　All the world's a stage,
And all the men and women merely players ;　　　140
They have their exits and their entrances ;
And one man in his time plays many parts,
His acts being seven ages. At first the infant,
Mewling and puking in the nurse's arms ;
Then the whining school-boy, with his satchel　　　145
And shining morning face, creeping like snail
Unwillingly to school. And then the lover,
Sighing like furnace, with a woeful ballad
Made to his mistress' eyebrow. Then a soldier,
Full of strange oaths, and bearded like the pard,　　　150
Jealous in honour, sudden and quick in quarrel,
Seeking the bubble reputation
Even in the cannon's mouth. And then the justice,
In fair round belly with good capon lin'd,
With eyes severe and beard of formal cut,　　　155
Full of wise saws and modern instances ,
And so he plays his part. The sixth age shifts
Into the lean and slipper'd pantaloon,
With spectacles on nose and pouch on side,
His youthful hose, well sav'd, a world too wide　　　160
For his shrunk shank ; and his big manly voice,
Turning again toward childish treble, pipes
And whistles in his sound. Last scene of all,
That ends this strange eventful history,
Is second childishness and mere oblivion ;　　　165
Sans teeth, sans eyes, sans taste, sans every thing.

Re-enter ORLANDO *with* ADAM.

DUKE S. Welcome. Set down your venerable burden.
And let him feed.
ORL. I thank you most for him.

Lines 121–123 omitted.

ADAM.   So had you need ;
  I scarce can speak to thank you for myself.   170
DUKE S. Welcome ; fall to.   I will not trouble you
  As yet to question you about your fortunes.
  Give us some music ; and, good cousin, sing.

Song.
  Blow, blow, thou winter wind,
  Thou art not so unkind   175
    As man's ingratitude ;
  Thy tooth is not so keen,
  Because thou art not seen,
    Although thy breath be rude.
Heigh-ho ! sing heigh-ho ! unto the green holly.   180
Most friendship is feigning, most loving mere folly.
  Then, heigh-ho, the holly !
    This life is most jolly.

  Freeze, freeze, thou bitter sky,
  That dost not bite so nigh   185
    As benefits forgot ;
  Though thou the waters warp,
  Thy sting is not so sharp
    As friend rememb'red not.
Heigh-ho ! sing, &c.   190

DUKE S. If that you were the good Sir Rowland's son,
  As you have whisper'd faithfully you were,
  And as mine eye doth his effigies witness
  Most truly limn'd and living in your face,
  Be truly welcome hither.   I am the Duke   195
  That lov'd your father.   The residue of your fortune,
  Go to my cave and tell me.   Good old man,
  Thou art right welcome as thy master is.
  Support him by the arm.   Give me your hand,
  And let me all your fortunes understand.   [*exeunt.*   Lines 199–200 omitted.

ACT THREE.

SCENE I.   *The palace.*

Enter DUKE FREDERICK, OLIVER, *and* LORDS.

DUKE F. Not see him since !   Sir, sir, that cannot be.
  But were I not the better part made mercy,
  I should not seek an absent argument
  Of my revenge, thou present.   But look to it :
  Find out thy brother wheresoe'er he is ;   5
  Seek him with candle ; bring him dead or living
  Within this twelvemonth, or turn thou no more
  To seek a living in our territory.
  Thy lands and all things that thou dost call thine
  Worth seizure do we seize into our hands,   10
  Till thou canst quit thee by thy brother's mouth
  Of what we think against thee.
OLI. O that your Highness knew my heart in this !
  I never lov'd my brother in my life.

SCENE 14
Interior. A Room in the Duke's Palace. Night.

DUKE F. More villain thou. Well, push him out of doors ;   15
And let my officers of such a nature
Make an extent upon his house and lands.
Do this expediently, and turn him going.   [exeunt.

SCENE II. *The forest.*

Enter ORLANDO, *with a paper.*

ORL. Hang there, my verse, in witness of my love ;
And thou, thrice-crowned Queen of Night, survey
With thy chaste eye, from thy pale sphere above,
Thy huntress' name that my full life doth sway.
O Rosalind ! these trees shall be my books,   5
And in their barks my thoughts I'll character,
That every eye which in this forest looks
Shall see thy virtue witness'd every where.
Run, run, Orlando ; carve on every tree,   9
The fair, the chaste, and unexpressive she.   [exit.

Enter CORIN *and* TOUCHSTONE.

COR. And how like you this shepherd's life, Master Touchstone ?
TOUCH. Truly, shepherd, in respect of itself, it is a good life ; but
in respect that it is a shepherd's life, it is nought. In respect
that it is solitary, I like it very well ; but in respect that it is
private, it is a very vile life. Now in respect it is in the fields,
it pleaseth me well ; but in respect it is not in the court, it is
tedious. As it is a spare life, look you, it fits my humour well ;
but as there is no more plenty in it, it goes much against my
stomach. Hast any philosophy in thee, shepherd ?   21
COR. No more but that I know the more one sickens the worse at
ease he is ; and that he that wants money, means, and content,
is without three good friends ; that the property of rain is to
wet, and fire to burn ; that good pasture makes fat sheep ; and
that a great cause of the night is lack of the sun ; that he that hath
learned no wit by nature nor art may complain of good breeding,
or comes of a very dull kindred.
TOUCH. Such a one is a natural philosopher. Wast ever in court,
shepherd ?   30
COR. No, truly.
TOUCH. Then thou art damn'd.
COR. Nay, I hope.
TOUCH. Truly, thou art damn'd, like an ill-roasted egg, all on one
side.   35
COR. For not being at court ? Your reason.
TOUCH. Why, if thou never wast at court thou never saw'st good
manners ; if thou never saw'st good manners, then thy manners
must be wicked ; and wickedness is sin, and sin is damnation.
Thou art in a parlous state, shepherd.
COR. Not a whit, Touchstone. Those that are good manners at the
court are as ridiculous in the country as the behaviour of the
country is most mockable at the court. You told me you salute
not at the court, but you kiss your hands ; that courtesy would
be uncleanly if courtiers were shepherds.
TOUCH. Instance, briefly ; come, instance.   46

COR. Why, we are still handling our ewes ; and their fells, you know,
are greasy.

TOUCH. Why, do not your courtier's hands sweat ? And is not the
grease of a mutton as wholesome as the sweat of a man ? Shallow,
shallow. A better instance, I say ; come.

COR. Besides, our hands are hard.   52

TOUCH. Your lips will feel them the sooner. Shallow again. A
more sounder instance ; come.

COR. And they are often tarr'd over with the surgery of our sheep ;
and would you have us kiss tar ? The courtier's hands are
perfum'd with civet.   57

TOUCH. Most shallow man ! thou worm's meat in respect of a good
piece of flesh indeed ! Learn of the wise, and perpend : civet
is of a baser birth than tar—the very uncleanly flux of a cat.
Mend the instance, shepherd.   61

COR. You have too courtly a wit for me ; I'll rest.

TOUCH. Wilt thou rest damn'd ? God help thee, shallow man !
God make incision in thee ! thou art raw.   64

COR. Sir, I am a true labourer : I earn that I eat, get that I wear ;
owe no man hate, envy no man's happiness ; glad of other men's
good, content with my harm ; and the greatest of my pride is to
see my ewes graze and my lambs suck.   68

TOUCH. That is another simple sin in you : to bring the ewes and
the rams together, and to offer to get your living by the copulation
of cattle ; to be bawd to a bell-wether, and to betray a she-lamb
of a twelvemonth to a crooked-pated, old, cuckoldly ram, out of
all reasonable match. If thou beest not damn'd for this, the
devil himself will have no shepherds ; I cannot see else how
thou shouldst scape.   75

COR. Here comes young Master Ganymede, my new mistress's
brother.

Enter ROSALIND, *reading a paper.*

ROS.   ' From the east to western Inde,
             No jewel is like Rosalinde.
             Her worth, being mounted on the wind,   80
             Through all the world bears Rosalinde.
             All the pictures fairest lin'd
             Are but black to Rosalinde.
             Let no face be kept in mind
             But the fair of Rosalinde.'   85

TOUCH. I'll rhyme you so eight years together, dinners, and suppers,
and sleeping hours, excepted. It is the right butter-women's
rank to market.

ROS. Out, fool !

TOUCH. For a taste :   90
             If a hart do lack a hind,
             Let him seek out Rosalinde.
             If the cat will after kind,
             So be sure will Rosalinde.
             Winter garments must be lin'd,   95
             So must slender Rosalinde.
             They that reap must sheaf and bind,
             Then to cart with Rosalinde.

Lines 71, 'to be bawd
. . .', to 77 omitted.

SCENE 17
*Exterior. A sheep field
near the Forest of
Arden. Day.*
ROSALIND,
TOUCHSTONE

Helen Mirren as Rosalind

<blockquote>
Sweetest nut hath sourest rind,
Such a nut is Rosalinde.   100
He that sweetest rose will find
Must find love's prick and Rosalinde.
</blockquote>

This is the very false gallop of verses ; why do you infect yourself with them ?

ROS. Peace, you dull fool !   I found them on a tree. 105

TOUCH. Truly, the tree yields bad fruit.

ROS. I'll graff it with you, and then I shall graff it with a medlar. Then it will be the earliest fruit i' th' country ; for you'll be rotten ere you be half ripe, and that's the right virtue of the medlar.   110

TOUCH. You have said ; but whether wisely or no, let the forest judge.

Enter CELIA, *with a writing.*

ROS. Peace !
Here comes my sister, reading ; stand aside.

CEL. ' Why should this a desert be ?   115
<blockquote>
 For it is unpeopled ? No ;
Tongues I'll hang on every tree
 That shall civil sayings show.
Some, how brief the life of man
 Runs his erring pilgrimage,   120
That the stretching of a span
 Buckles in his sum of age ;
Some, of violated vows
 'Twixt the souls of friend and friend ;
But upon the fairest boughs,   125
 Or at every sentence end,
Will I Rosalinda write,
 Teaching all that read to know
The quintessence of every sprite
 Heaven would in little show.   130
Therefore heaven Nature charg'd
 That one body should be fill'd
With all graces wide-enlarg'd.
 Nature presently distill'd
Helen's cheek, but not her heart,   135
 Cleopatra's majesty,
Atalanta's better part,
 Sad Lucretia's modesty.
Thus Rosalinde of many parts
 By heavenly synod was devis'd,   140
Of many faces, eyes, and hearts,
 To have the touches dearest priz'd.
Heaven would that she these gifts should have,
 And I to live and die her slave.'   144
</blockquote>

Lines 119–124 omitted.

ROS. O most gentle pulpiter !   What tedious homily of love have you wearied your parishioners withal, and never cried ' Have patience, good people'.

CEL. How now !   Back, friends ; shepherd, go off a little ; go with him, sirrah.   149

TOUCH. Come, shepherd, let us make an honourable retreat ; though not with bag and baggage yet with scrip and scrippage.

[*exeunt* CORIN *and* TOUCHSTONE.

CEL. Didst thou hear these verses?   153
ROS. O, yes, I heard them all, and more too ; for some of them had
    in them more feet than the verses would bear.
CEL. That's no matter ; the feet might bear the verses.   'That's no matter . . .
ROS. Ay, but the feet were lame, and could not bear themselves in the verse' omitted.
    without the verse, and therefore stood lamely in the verse.   159
CEL. But didst thou hear without wondering how thy name should
    be hang'd and carved upon these trees?
ROS. I was seven of the nine days out of the wonder before you came ;
    for look here what I found on a palm-tree. I was never so
    berhym'd since Pythagoras' time that I was an Irish rat, which
    I can hardly remember.   165
CEL. Trow you who hath done this?
ROS. Is it a man?
CEL. And a chain, that you once wore, about his neck. Change you
    colour?
ROS. I prithee, who?   170
CEL. O Lord, Lord! it is a hard matter for friends to meet ; but
    mountains may be remov'd with earthquakes, and so encounter.
ROS. Nay, but who is it?
CEL. Is it possible?
ROS. Nay, I prithee now, with most petitionary vehemence, tell me
    who it is.
CEL. O wonderful, wonderful, and most wonderful wonderful, and
    yet again wonderful, and after that, out of all whooping!   180
ROS. Good my complexion! dost thou think, though I am caparison'd
    like a man, I have a doublet and hose in my disposition? One
    inch of delay more is a South Sea of discovery. I prithee tell
    me who is it quickly, and speak apace. I would thou could'st 'I would thou . . .
    stammer, that thou mightst pour this conceal'd man out of thy none at all' omitted.
    mouth, as wine comes out of a narrow-mouth'd bottle—either
    too much at once or none at all. I prithee take the cork out of
    thy mouth that I may drink thy tidings.
CEL. So you may put a man in your belly.   190
ROS. Is he of God's making? What manner of man? Is his head
    worth a hat or his chin worth a beard?
CEL. Nay, he hath but a little beard.
ROS. Why, God will send more if the man will be thankful. Let
    me stay the growth of his beard, if thou delay me not the know-
    ledge of his chin.   196
CEL. It is young Orlando, that tripp'd up the wrestler's heels and
    your heart both in an instant.
ROS. Nay, but the devil take mocking! Speak sad brow and true
    maid.   200
CEL. I' faith, coz, 'tis he.
ROS. Orlando?
CEL. Orlando.
ROS. Alas the day! what shall I do with my doublet and hose?
    What did he when thou saw'st him? What said he? How
    look'd he? Wherein went he? What makes he here? Did he
    ask for me? Where remains he? How parted he with thee?
    And when shalt thou see him again? Answer me in one word.

CEL. You must borrow me Gargantua's mouth first; 'tis a word too
great for any mouth of this age's size. To say ay and no to these
particulars is more than to answer in a catechism. 213

'To say ay . . . in a
catechism' omitted.

ROS. But doth he know that I am in this forest, and in man's apparel?
Looks he as freshly as he did the day he wrestled?
CEL. It is as easy to count atomies as to resolve the propositions of
a lover; but take a taste of my finding him, and relish it with
good observance. I found him under a tree, like a dropp'd acorn.
ROS. It may well be call'd Jove's tree, when it drops forth such fruit.
CEL. Give me audience, good madam. 222
ROS. Proceed.
CEL. There lay he, stretch'd along like a wounded knight.
ROS. Though it be pity to see such a sight, it well becomes the ground.
CEL. Cry ' Holla ' to thy tongue, I prithee; it curvets unseasonably.
He was furnish'd like a hunter. 230
ROS. O, ominous! he comes to kill my heart.
CEL. I would sing my song without a burden; thou bring'st me out
of tune.
ROS. Do you not know I am a woman? When I think, I must
speak. Sweet, say on. 235
CEL. You bring me out. Soft! comes he not here?

Enter ORLANDO *and* JAQUES.

ORLANDO *and* JAQUES
enter one line later.

ROS. 'Tis he; slink by, and note him.
JAQ. I thank you for your company; but, good faith, I had as lief
have been myself alone.
ORL. And so had I; but yet, for fashion sake, I thank you too for
your society. 241

SCENE 18
*Exterior. An Oak
Wood in the Forest of
Arden. Day.*
ROSALIND, CELIA,
ORLANDO, JAQUES

JAQ. God buy you; let's meet as little as we can.
ORL. I do desire we may be better strangers.
JAQ. I pray you mar no more trees with writing love songs in their
barks. 245
ORL. I pray you mar no more of my verses with reading them ill-
favouredly.
JAQ. Rosalind is your love's name?
ORL. Yes, just.
JAQ. I do not like her name. 250
ORL. There was no thought of pleasing you when she was christen'd.
JAQ. What stature is she of?
ORL. Just as high as my heart.
JAQ. You are full of pretty answers. Have you not been acquainted
with goldsmiths' wives, and conn'd them out of rings?
ORL. Not so; but I answer you right painted cloth, from whence
you have studied your questions. 259
JAQ. You have a nimble wit; I think 'twas made of Atalanta's heels.
Will you sit down with me? and we two will rail against our
mistress the world, and all our misery.
ORL. I will chide no breather in the world but myself, against whom
I know most faults.
JAQ. The worst fault you have is to be in love. 265
ORL. 'Tis a fault I will not change for your best virtue. I am weary
of you.
JAQ. By my troth, I was seeking for a fool when I found you.
ORL. He is drown'd in the brook; look but in, and you shall see him.

JAQ. There I shall see mine own figure.   272
ORL. Which I take to be either a fool or a cipher.
JAQ. I'll tarry no longer with you ; farewell, good Signior Love.
ORL. I am glad of your departure ; adieu, good Monsieur Melancholy.
                                                    [*exit* JAQUES.
ROS. [*aside to* CELIA.]   I will speak to him like a saucy lackey, and
    under that habit play the knave with him.—Do you hear, forester ?
ORL. Very well ; what would you ?   281
ROS. I pray you, what is't o'clock ?
ORL. You should ask me what time o' day ; there's no clock in the
    forest.
ROS. Then there is no true lover in the forest, else sighing every
    minute and groaning every hour would detect the lazy foot of
    Time as well as a clock.   287
ORL. And why not the swift foot of Time ?   Had not that been as
    proper ?
ROS. By no means, sir.   Time travels in divers paces with divers
    persons.   I'll tell you who Time ambles withal, who Time trots
    withal, who Time gallops withal, and who he stands still withal.
ORL. I prithee, who doth he trot withal ?   294
ROS. Marry, he trots hard with a young maid between the contract
    of her marriage and the day it is solemnized ; if the interim be
    but a se'nnight, Time's pace is so hard that it seems the length
    of seven year.
ORL. Who ambles Time withal ?   299
ROS. With a priest that lacks Latin and a rich man that hath not the
    gout ; for the one sleeps easily because he cannot study, and
    the other lives merrily because he feels no pain ; the one lacking the
    burden of lean and wasteful learning, the other knowing no
    burden of heavy tedious penury.   These Time ambles withal.
ORL. Who doth he gallop withal ?   306
ROS. With a thief to the gallows ; for though he go as softly as foot
    can fall, he thinks himself too soon there.
ORL. Who stays it still withal ?
ROS. With lawyers in the vacation ; for they sleep between term
    and term, and then they perceive not how Time moves.
ORL. Where dwell you, pretty youth ?
ROS. With this shepherdess, my sister ; here in the skirts of the
    forest, like fringe upon a petticoat.   315
ORL. Are you native of this place ?
ROS. As the coney that you see dwell where she is kindled.
ORL. Your accent is something finer than you could purchase in so
    removed a dwelling.
ROS. I have been told so of many ; but indeed an old religious uncle
    of mine taught me to speak, who was in his youth an inland man ;
    one that knew courtship too well, for there he fell in love.   I
    have heard him read many lectures against it ; and I thank God
    I am not a woman, to be touch'd with so many giddy offences
    as he hath generally tax'd their whole sex withal.   326
ORL. Can you remember any of the principal evils that he laid to
    the charge of women ?
ROS. There were none principal ; they were all like one another as
    halfpence are ; every one fault seeming monstrous till his fellow-
    fault came to match it.   331

ORL. I prithee recount some of them.

ROS. No ; I will not cast away my physic but on those that are sick. There is a man haunts the forest that abuses our young plants with carving ' Rosalind ' on their barks ; hangs odes upon hawthorns and elegies on brambles ; all, forsooth, deifying the name of Rosalind. If I could meet that fancy-monger, I would give him some good counsel, for he seems to have the quotidian of love upon him.   339

ORL. I am he that is so love-shak'd ; I pray you tell me your remedy.

ROS. There is none of my uncle's marks upon you ; he taught me how to know a man in love ; in which cage of rushes I am sure you are not prisoner.

ORL. What were his marks ?   345

ROS. A lean cheek, which you have not ; a blue eye and sunken, which you have not ; an unquestionable spirit, which you have not ; a beard neglected, which you have not ; but I pardon you for that, for simply your having in beard is a younger brother's revenue. Then your hose should be ungarter'd, your bonnet unbanded, your sleeve unbutton'd, your shoe untied, and every thing about you demonstrating a careless desolation. But you are no such man ; you are rather point-device in your accoutrements, as loving yourself than seeming the lover of any other.

ORL. Fair youth, I would I could make thee believe I love.   357

ROS. Me believe it ! You may as soon make her that you love believe it ; which, I warrant, she is apter to do than to confess she does. That is one of the points in the which women still give the lie to their consciences. But, in good sooth, are you he that hangs the verses on the trees wherein Rosalind is so admired ?

ORL. I swear to thee, youth, by the white hand of Rosalind, I am that he, that unfortunate he.   365

ROS. But are you so much in love as your rhymes speak ?

ORL. Neither rhyme nor reason can express how much.

ROS. Love is merely a madness ; and, I tell you, deserves as well a dark house and a whip as madmen do ; and the reason why they are not so punish'd and cured is that the lunacy is so ordinary that the whippers are in love too. Yet I profess curing it by counsel.   372

ORL. Did you ever cure any so ?

ROS. Yes, one ; and in this manner. He was to imagine me his love, his mistress ; and I set him every day to woo me ; at which time would I being but a moonish youth, grieve, be effeminate, changeable, longing and liking, proud, fantastical, apish, shallow, inconstant, full of tears, full of smiles ; for every passion something and for no passion truly anything, as boys and women are for the most part cattle of this colour ; would now like him, now loathe him ; then entertain him, then forswear him ; now weep for him, then spit at him ; that I drave my suitor from his mad humour of love to a living humour of madness ; which was, to forswear the full stream of the world and to live in a nook merely monastic. And thus I cur'd him ; and this way will I take upon me to wash your liver as clean as a sound sheep's heart, that there shall not be one spot of love in 't.

ORL. I would not be cured, youth.   389

ROS. I would cure you, if you would but call me Rosalind, and come
     every day to my cote and woo me.
ORL. Now, by the faith of my love, I will. Tell me where it is.
ROS. Go with me to it, and I'll show it you ; and, by the way, you
     shall tell me where in the forest you live. Will you go ?   396
ORL. With all my heart, good youth.
ROS. Nay, you must call me Rosalind. Come, sister, will you go ?
                                                          [*exeunt.*

SCENE III. *The forest.*

Enter TOUCHSTONE *and* AUDREY ; JAQUES *behind.*

SCENE 19
Exterior. A sheep field
near the Forest of
Arden. Day.

TOUCH. Come apace, good Audrey ; I will fetch up your goats,
     Audrey. And how, Audrey, am I the man yet ? Doth my
     simple feature content you ?
AUD. Your features ! Lord warrant us ! What features ?
TOUCH. I am here with thee and thy goats, as the most capricious
     poet, honest Ovid, was among the Goths.   6
JAQ. [*aside.*] O knowledge ill-inhabited, worse than Jove in a
     thatch'd house !
TOUCH. When a man's verses cannot be understood, nor a man's
     good wit seconded with the forward child understanding, it strikes
     a man more dead than a great reckoning in a little room. Truly,
     I would the gods had made thee poetical.
AUD. I do not know what ' poetical ' is. Is it honest in deed and
     word ? Is it a true thing ?   15
TOUCH. No, truly ; for the truest poetry is the most feigning, and
     lovers are given to poetry ; and what they swear in poetry may
     be said as lovers they do feign.
AUD. Do you wish, then, that the gods had made me poetical ?   20
TOUCH. I do, truly, for thou swear'st to me thou art honest ; now,
     if thou wert a poet, I might have some hope thou didst feign.
AUD. Would you not have me honest ?
TOUCH. No, truly, unless thou wert hard-favour'd ; for honesty
     coupled to beauty is to have honey a sauce to sugar.
JAQ. [*aside.*] A material fool !
AUD. Well, I am not fair ; and therefore I pray the gods make me
     honest.   30
TOUCH. Truly, and to cast away honesty upon a foul slut were to
     put good meat into an unclean dish.
AUD. I am not a slut, though I thank the gods I am foul.   34
TOUCH. Well, praised be the gods for thy foulness ; sluttishness may
     come hereafter. But be it as it may be, I will marry thee ; and
     to that end I have been with Sir Oliver Martext, the vicar of the
     next village, who hath promis'd to meet me in this place of the
     forest, and to couple us.
JAQ. [*aside.*] I would fain see this meeting.   40
AUD. Well, the gods give us joy !
TOUCH. Amen. A man may, if he were of a fearful heart, stagger
     in this attempt ; for here we have no temple but the wood, no
     assembly but horn-beasts. But what though ? Courage ! As
     horns are odious, they are necessary. It is said : ' Many a man
     knows no end of his goods'. Right ! Many a man has good
     horns and knows no end of them. Well, that is the dowry of

'It is said . . . dowry
of' omitted.

his wife ; 'tis none of his own getting. Horns ? Even so. Poor
men alone ? No, no ; the noblest deer hath them as huge as
the rascal. Is the single man therefore blessed ? No ; as a
wall'd town is more worthier than a village, so is the forehead
of a married man more honourable than the bare brow of a
bachelor ; and by how much defence is better than no skill, by
so much is a horn more precious than to want. Here comes
Sir Oliver.   55

'his wife . . .
therefore blessed'
omitted.

'and by how . . . Sir
Oliver' omitted.

Enter SIR OLIVER MARTEXT.

Sir Oliver Martext, you are well met. Will you dispatch us here
under this tree, or shall we go with you to your chapel ?
SIR OLI. Is there none here to give the woman ?
TOUCH. I will not take her on gift of any man.   60
SIR OLI. Truly, she must be given, or the marriage is not lawful.
JAQ. [*discovering himself.*]   Proceed, proceed ; I'll give her.
TOUCH. Good even, good Master What-ye-call't ; how do you, sir ?
You are very well met. Goddild you for your last company. I
am very glad to see you. Even a toy in hand here, sir. Nay ;
pray be cover'd.   67

'Goddild you for your
last company'
omitted.

JAQ. Will you be married, motley ?
TOUCH. As the ox hath his bow, sir, the horse his curb, and the
falcon her bells, so man hath his desires ; and as pigeons bill,
so wedlock would be nibbling.   71
JAQ. And will you, being a man of your breeding, be married under
a bush, like a beggar ? Get you to church and have a good
priest that can tell you what marriage is ; this fellow will but
join you together as they join wainscot ; then one of you will
prove a shrunk panel, and like green timber warp, warp.   77
TOUCH. [*aside.*]   I am not in the mind but I were better to be married
of him than of another ; for he is not like to marry me well ;
and not being well married, it will be a good excuse for me hereafter to leave my wife.   81
JAQ. Go thou with me, and let me counsel thee.
TOUCH. Come, sweet Audrey ;
We must be married or we must live in bawdry.
Farewell, good Master Oliver. Not—   85
           O sweet Oliver,
           O brave Oliver,
    Leave me not behind thee.
But—
           Wind away,   90
           Begone, I say,
    I will not to wedding with thee.
                   [*exeunt* JAQUES, TOUCHSTONE, *and* AUDREY.
SIR OLI. 'Tis no matter ; ne'er a fantastical knave of them all shall
flout me out of my calling.   [*exit.*

SCENE IV.   *The forest.*

Enter ROSALIND *and* CELIA.

ROS. Never talk to me ; I will weep.
CEL. Do, I prithee ; but yet have the grace to consider that tears
do not become a man.

SCENE 20
*Exterior. Beneath a
large Chestnut Tree in
the Forest of Arden.
Day.*

Angharad Rees as Celia and Helen Mirren as Rosalind

From left to right: Jaques (Richard Pasco), Touchstone (James Bolam), the Banished Duke (Tony Church) and Oliver (Clive Francis)

ROS. But have I not cause to weep?
CEL. As good cause as one would desire; therefore weep.
ROS. His very hair is of the dissembling colour.   6
CEL. Something browner than Judas's.
       Marry, his kisses are Judas's own children.
ROS. I'faith, his hair is of a good colour.
CEL. An excellent colour: your chestnut was ever the only colour.
ROS. And his kissing is as full of sanctity as the touch of holy bread.
| CEL. He hath bought a pair of cast lips of Diana. A nun of winter's | 'He hath bought a
       sisterhood kisses not more religiously; the very ice of chastity   pair of cast lips of
       is in them.   16   Diana' omitted.
ROS. But why did he swear he would come this morning, and comes
       not?
CEL. Nay, certainly, there is no truth in him.
ROS. Do you think so?   20   Lines 20–23 omitted.
CEL. Yes; I think he is not a pick-purse nor a horse-stealer; but
       for his verity in love, I do think him as concave as a covered
       goblet or a worm-eaten nut.
ROS. Not true in love?
CEL. Yes, when he is in; but I think he is not in.   25
ROS. You have heard him swear downright he was.
CEL. 'Was' is not 'is'; besides, the oath of a lover is no stronger
       than the word of a tapster; they are both the confirmer of false
       reckonings. He attends here in the forest on the Duke, your
       father.   30
ROS. I met the Duke yesterday, and had much question with him.
       He asked me of what parentage I was; I told him, of as good as
       he; so he laugh'd and let me go. But what talk we of fathers
       when there is such a man as Orlando?   35
CEL. O, that's a brave man! He writes brave verses, speaks brave
       words, swears brave oaths, and breaks them bravely, quite
       traverse, athwart the heart of his lover; as a puny tilter, that   'as a puny tilter . . .
       spurs his horse but on one side, breaks his staff like a noble   noble goose' omitted.
       goose. But all's brave that youth mounts and folly guides.
       Who comes here?   41   'Who comes here?'
                                                                            omitted.
                          Enter CORIN.

COR. Mistress and master, you have oft enquired
       After the shepherd that complain'd of love,
       Who you saw sitting by me on the turf, | Line 44 omitted.
       Praising the proud disdainful shepherdess   45
       That was his mistress.
CEL.   Well, and what of him?
COR. If you will see a pageant truly play'd
       Between the pale complexion of true love
       And the red glow of scorn and proud disdain,
       Go hence a little, and I shall conduct you,   50
       If you will mark it.
ROS.   O, come, let us remove!
       The sight of lovers feedeth those in love.
       Bring us to this sight, and you shall say | Lines 53–54 omitted.
       I'll prove a busy actor in their play.   [*exeunt.*

SCENE V. *Another part of the forest.*

Enter SILVIUS *and* PHEBE.

SCENE 21
*Exterior. An Oak
Wood in the Forest of
Arden. Day.*

SIL. Sweet Phebe, do not scorn me ; do not, Phebe.
Say that you love me not ; but say not so
In bitterness.   The common executioner,
Whose heart th' accustom'd sight of death makes hard,
Falls not the axe upon the humbled neck   5
But first begs pardon.   Will you sterner be
Than he that dies and lives by bloody drops ?

Enter ROSALIND, CELIA, *and* CORIN, *at a distance.*

PHE. I would not be thy executioner ;
I fly thee, for I would not injure thee.
Thou tell'st me there is murder in mine eye.   10
'Tis pretty, sure, and very probable,
That eyes, that are the frail'st and softest things,
Who shut their coward gates on atomies,
Should be call'd tyrants, butchers, murderers !
Now I do frown on thee with all my heart ;   15
And if mine eyes can wound, now let them kill thee.
Now counterfeit to swoon ; why, now fall down ;
Or, if thou canst not, O, for shame, for shame,
Lie not, to say mine eyes are murderers.
Now show the wound mine eye hath made in thee.   20
Scratch thee but with a pin, and there remains
Some scar of it ; lean upon a rush,
The cicatrice and capable impressure
Thy palm some moment keeps ; but now mine eyes,
Which I have darted at thee, hurt thee not ;   25
Nor, I am sure, there is not force in eyes
That can do hurt.
SIL.   O dear Phebe,
If ever—as that ever may be near—
You meet in some fresh cheek the power of fancy,
Then shall you know the wounds invisible   30
That love's keen arrows make.
PHE.   But till that time
Come not thou near me ; and when that time comes,
Afflict me with thy mocks, pity me not ;
As till that time I shall not pity thee.   34
ROS. [*advancing.*] And why, I pray you ? Who might be your mother,
That you insult, exult, and all at once,
Over the wretched ?   What though you have no beauty—
As, by my faith, I see no more in you
Than without candle may go dark to bed—
Must you be therefore proud and pitiless ?   40
Why, what means this ?   Why do you look on me ?
I see no more in you than in the ordinary
Of nature's sale-work.   'Od's my little life,
I think she means to tangle my eyes too !
No faith, proud mistress, hope not after it ;   45
'Tis not your inky brows, your black silk hair,

Lines 21–25 omitted.

Your bugle eyeballs, nor your cheek of cream,
That can entame my spirits to your worship.
You foolish shepherd, wherefore do you follow her,
Like foggy south, puffing with wind and rain ?   50
You are a thousand times a properer man
Than she a woman. 'Tis such fools as you
That makes the world full of ill-favour'd children.
'Tis not her glass, but you, that flatters her ;
And out of you she sees herself more proper   55
Than any of her lineaments can show her.
But, mistress, know yourself. Down on your knees,
And thank heaven, fasting, for a good man's love ;
For I must tell you friendly in your ear :
Sell when you can ; you are not for all markets.   60
Cry the man mercy, love him, take his offer ;
Foul is most foul, being foul to be a scoffer.
So take her to thee, shepherd. Fare you well.
PHE. Sweet youth, I pray you chide a year together ;
I had rather hear you chide than this man woo.   65
ROS. He's fall'n in love with your foulness, and she'll fall in love
with my anger. If it be so, as fast as she answers thee with
frowning looks, I'll sauce her with bitter words. Why look you
so upon me ?
PHE. For no ill will I bear you.   70
ROS. I pray you do not fall in love with me,
For I am falser than vows made in wine ;
Besides, I like you not. If you will know my house,
'Tis at the tuft of olives here hard by.
Will you go, sister ? Shepherd, ply her hard.   75
Come, sister. Shepherdess, look on him better,
And be not proud ; though all the world could see,
None could be so abus'd in sight as he.
Come, to our flock.   [exeunt ROSALIND, CELIA, and CORIN.
PHE. Dead shepherd, now I find thy saw of might :   80
' Who ever lov'd that lov'd not at first sight ? '
SIL. Sweet Phebe.
PHE.   Ha ! what say'st thou, Silvius ?
SIL. Sweet Phebe, pity me.
PHE. Why, I am sorry for thee, gentle Silvius.
SIL. Wherever sorrow is, relief would be.   85
If you do sorrow at my grief in love,
By giving love, your sorrow and my grief
Were both extermin'd.
PHE. Thou hast my love ; is not that neighbourly ?
SIL. I would have you.
PHE.   Why, that were covetousness.   90
Silvius, the time was that I hated thee ;
And yet it is not that I bear thee love ;
But since that thou canst talk of love so well,
Thy company, which erst was irksome to me,
I will endure ; and I'll employ thee too.   95
But do not look for further recompense
Than thine own gladness that thou art employ'd.

SIL. So holy and so perfect is my love,
  And I in such a poverty of grace,
  That I shall think it a most plenteous crop   100
  To glean the broken ears after the man
  That the main harvest reaps ; loose now and then
  A scatt'red smile, and that I'll live upon.
PHE. Know'st thou the youth that spoke to me erewhile ?
SIL. Not very well ; but I have met him oft ;   105
  And he hath bought the cottage and the bounds
  That the old carlot once was master of.
PHE. Think not I love him, though I ask for him ;
  'Tis but a peevish boy ; yet he talks well.
  But what care I for words ?   Yet words do well   110
  When he that speaks them pleases those that hear.
  It is a pretty youth—not very pretty ;
  But, sure, he's proud ; and yet his pride becomes him.
  He'll make a proper man.   The best thing in him
  Is his complexion ; and faster than his tongue   115
  Did make offence, his eye did heal it up.
  He is not very tall ; yet for his years he's tall ;
  His leg is but so-so ; and yet 'tis well.
  There was a pretty redness in his lip,
  A little riper and more lusty red   120
  Than that mix'd in his cheek ; 'twas just the difference
  Betwixt the constant red and mingled damask.
  There be some women, Silvius, had they mark'd him
  In parcels as I did, would have gone near
  To fall in love with him ; but, for my part,   125
  I love him not, nor hate him not ; and yet
  I have more cause to hate him than to love him ;
  For what had he to do to chide at me ?
  He said mine eyes were black, and my hair black,
  And, now I am rememb'red, scorn'd at me.   130
  I marvel why I answer'd not again ;
  But that's all one : omittance is no quittance.
  I'll write to him a very taunting letter,
  And thou shalt bear it ; wilt thou, Silvius ?
SIL. Phebe, with all my heart.
PHE.   I'll write it straight ;   135
  The matter's in my head and in my heart ;
  I will be bitter with him and passing short.
  Go with me, Silvius.   [exeunt.

ACT FOUR.

SCENE I.   The forest.

Enter ROSALIND, CELIA, *and* JAQUES.

SCENE 22
*Exterior. Beneath a
large Chestnut Tree in
the Forest of Arden.
Day.*

JAQ. I prithee, pretty youth, let me be better acquainted with thee.
ROS. They say you are a melancholy fellow.
JAQ. I am so ; I do love it better than laughing.
ROS. Those that are in extremity of either are abominable fellows,
  and betray themselves to every modern censure worse than
  drunkards.

JAQ. Why, 'tis good to be sad and say nothing.
ROS. Why then, 'tis good to be a post.   9
JAQ. I have neither the scholar's melancholy, which is emulation;
nor the musician's, which is fantastical ; nor the courtier's, which
is proud ; nor the soldier's, which is ambitious ; nor the lawyer's,
which is politic ; nor the lady's, which is nice ; nor the lover's,
which is all these ; but it is a melancholy of mine own, com-
pounded of many simples, extracted from many objects, and,
indeed, the sundry contemplation of my travels ; in which my
often rumination wraps me in a most humorous sadness.   18
ROS. A traveller ! By my faith, you have great reason to be sad.
I fear you have sold your own lands to see other men's ; then
to have seen much and to have nothing is to have rich eyes and
poor hands.
JAQ. Yes, I have gain'd my experience.

Enter ORLANDO.

ROS. And your experience makes you sad. I had rather have a fool
to make me merry than experience to make me sad—and to travel
for it too.   26
ORL. Good day, and happiness, dear Rosalind !
JAQ. Nay, then, God buy you, an you talk in blank verse.
ROS. Farewell, Monsieur Traveller ; look you lisp and wear strange
suits, disable all the benefits of your own country, be out of love
with your nativity, and almost chide God for making you that
countenance you are ; or I will scarce think you have swam in
a gondola. [*exit* JAQUES.] Why, how now, Orlando ! where have
you been all this while ? You a lover ! An you serve me such
another trick, never come in my sight more.   37
ORL. My fair Rosalind, I come within an hour of my promise.
ROS. Break an hour's promise in love ! He that will divide a minute
into a thousand parts, and break but a part of the thousand part
of a minute in the affairs of love, it may be said of him that Cupid
hath clapp'd him o' th' shoulder, but I'll warrant him heart-whole.
ORL. Pardon me, dear Rosalind.   45
ROS. Nay, an you be so tardy, come no more in my sight. I had
as lief be woo'd of a snail.
ORL. Of a snail !
ROS. Ay, of a snail ; for though he comes slowly, he carries his house
on his head—a better jointure, I think, than you make a woman ;
besides, he brings his destiny with him.
ORL. What's that ?
ROS. Why, horns ; which such as you are fain to be beholding to
your wives for ; but he comes armed in his fortune, and prevents
the slander of his wife.   55
ORL. Virtue is no horn-maker ; and my Rosalind is virtuous.
ROS. And I am your Rosalind.
CEL. It pleases him to call you so ; but he hath a Rosalind of a better
leer than you.   60
ROS. Come, woo me, woo me ; for now I am in a holiday humour,
and like enough to consent. What would you say to me now,
an I were your very very Rosalind ?
ORL. I would kiss before I spoke.   64

'but he comes . . . his
wife' omitted.

ROS. Nay, you were better speak first ; and when you were gravell'd for lack of matter, you might take occasion to kiss. Very good orators, when they are out, they will spit ; and for lovers lacking— God warn us !—matter, the cleanliest shift is to kiss.
ORL. How if the kiss be denied ?   70
ROS. Then she puts you to entreaty, and there begins new matter.
ORL. Who could be out, being before his beloved mistress ?
ROS. Marry, that should you, if I were your mistress ; or I should think my honesty ranker than my wit.   75
ORL. What, of my suit ?
ROS. Not out of your apparel, and yet out of your suit. Am not I your Rosalind ?
ORL. I take some joy to say you are, because I would be talking of her.
ROS. Well, in her person, I say I will not have you.
ORL. Then, in mine own person, I die.   82
ROS. No, faith, die by attorney. The poor world is almost six thousand years old, and in all this time there was not any man died in his own person, videlicet, in a love-cause. Troilus had his brains dash'd out with a Grecian club ; yet he did what he could to die before, and he is one of the patterns of love. Leander, he would have liv'd many a fair year. though Hero had turn'd nun, if it had not been for a hot midsummer night ; for, good youth, he went but forth to wash him in the Hellespont, and, being taken with the cramp, was drown'd ; and the foolish chroniclers of that age found it was—Hero of Sestos. But these are all lies : men have died from time to time, and worms have eaten them, but not for love.   95
ORL. I would not have my right Rosalind of this mind ; for, I protest, her frown might kill me.
ROS. By this hand, it will not kill a fly. But come. now I will be your Rosalind in a more coming-on disposition ; and ask me what you will, I will grant it.   100
ORL. Then love me, Rosalind.
ROS. Yes, faith, will I, Fridays and Saturdays, and all.
ORL. And wilt thou have me ?
ROS. Ay, and twenty such.
ORL. What sayest thou ?   105
ROS. Are you not good ?
ORL. I hope so.
ROS. Why then, can one desire too much of a good thing ? Come, sister, you shall be the priest, and marry us. Give me your hand, Orlando. What do you say, sister ?   110
ORL. Pray thee, marry us.
CEL. I cannot say the words.
ROS. You must begin ' Will you, Orlando '—
CEL. Go to. Will you, Orlando, have to wife this Rosalind ?
ORL. I will.
ROS. Ay, but when ?
ORL. Why, now ; as fast as she can marry us.
ROS. Then you must say ' I take thee, Rosalind, for wife'.
ORL. I take thee, Rosalind, for wife.
ROS. I might ask you for your commission ; but—I do take thee, Orlando, for my husband. There's a girl goes before the priest ; and, certainly, a woman's thought runs before her actions. 125

Lines 72–75, 'who could . . . than my wit', omitted.

69

ORL. So do all thoughts; they are wing'd.

ROS. Now tell me how long you would have her, after you have possess'd her.

ORL. For ever and a day. 129

ROS. Say ' a day ' without the ' ever '. No, no, Orlando; men are April when they woo, December when they wed : maids are May when they are maids, but the sky changes when they are wives. I will be more jealous of thee than a Barbary cock-pigeon over his hen, more clamorous than a parrot against rain, more new-fangled than an ape, more giddy in my desires than a monkey. I will weep for nothing, like Diana in the fountain, and I will do that when you are dispos'd to be merry; I will laugh like a hyen, and that when thou art inclin'd to sleep.

ORL. But will my Rosalind do so ? 140

ROS. By my life, she will do as I do.

ORL. O, but she is wise.

ROS. Or else she could not have the wit to do this. The wiser, the waywarder. Make the doors upon a woman's wit, and it will out at the casement; shut that, and 'twill out at the key-hole; stop that, 'twill fly with the smoke out at the chimney. 147

ORL. A man that had a wife with such a wit, he might say ' Wit, whither wilt ? '

ROS. Nay, you might keep that check for it, till you met your wife's wit going to your neighbour's bed. 151

ORL. And what wit could wit have to excuse that ?

ROS. Marry, to say she came to seek you there. You shall never take her without her answer, unless you take her without her tongue. O, that woman that cannot make her fault her husband's occasion, let her never nurse her child herself, for she will breed it like a fool ! 157

ORL. For these two hours, Rosalind, I will leave thee.

ROS. Alas, dear love, I cannot lack thee two hours !

ORL. I must attend the Duke at dinner; by two o'clock I will be with thee again. 161

ROS. Ay, go your ways, go your ways. I knew what you would prove; my friends told me as much, and I thought no less. That flattering tongue of yours won me. 'Tis but one cast away, and so, come death ! Two o'clock is your hour ? 166

ORL. Ay, sweet Rosalind.

ROS. By my troth, and in good earnest, and so God mend me, and by all pretty oaths that are not dangerous, if you break one jot of your promise, or come one minute behind your hour, I will think you the most pathetical break-promise, and the most hollow lover, and the most unworthy of her you call Rosalind, that may be chosen out of the gross band of the unfaithful. Therefore beware my censure, and keep your promise. 175

ORL. With no less religion than if thou wert indeed my Rosalind; so, adieu.

ROS. Well, Time is the old justice that examines all such offenders, and let Time try. Adieu. [exit ORLANDO.

CEL. You have simply misus'd our sex in your love-prate. We must have your doublet and hose pluck'd over your head, and show the world what the bird hath done to her own nest. 183

ROS. O coz, coz, coz, my pretty little coz, that thou didst know how

Lines 148–157 omitted.

many fathom deep I am in love ! But it cannot be sounded ;
my affection hath an unknown bottom, like the Bay of Portugal.
CEL. Or rather, bottomless ; that as fast as you pour affection in,
it runs out.   189
ROS. No ; that same wicked bastard of Venus, that was begot of
thought, conceiv'd of spleen, and born of madness ; that blind
rascally boy, that abuses every one's eyes, because his own are
out—let him be judge how deep I am in love. I'll tell thee,
Aliena, I cannot be out of the sight of Orlando. I'll go find a
shadow, and sigh till he come.   195
CEL. And I'll sleep.   [*exeunt.*

SCENE II.   *The forest.*

Enter JAQUES *and* LORDS, *in the habit of foresters.*

	SCENE 23
	Exterior. Beneath a
	large Beech Tree in the
	Forest of Arden. Day.

JAQ. Which is he that killed the deer ?
LORD. Sir, it was I.
JAQ. Let's present him to the Duke, like a Roman conqueror ; and
it would do well to set the deer's horns upon his head for a branch
of victory. Have you no song, forester, for this purpose ?   6
LORD. Yes, sir.
JAQ. Sing it ; 'tis no matter how it be in tune, so it make noise enough.

Song.

What shall he have that kill'd the deer ?   10
His leather skin and horns to wear.
                [*the rest shall bear this burden :*
        Then sing him home.
Take thou no scorn to wear the horn ;
It was a crest ere thou wast born.
        Thy father's father wore it ;   15
        And thy father bore it.
The horn, the horn, the lusty horn,
Is not a thing to laugh to scorn.   [*exeunt.*

SCENE III.   *The forest.*

Enter ROSALIND *and* CELIA.

	SCENE 24
	Exterior. Beneath a
	large Chestnut Tree in
	the Forest of Arden.
	Day.

ROS. How say you now ? Is it not past two o'clock ? And here
much Orlando !
CEL. I warrant you, with pure love and troubled brain, he hath ta'en
his bow and arrows, and is gone forth—to sleep. Look, who
comes here.   5

'Look, who comes
here' omitted.

Enter SILVIUS.

SIL. My errand is to you, fair youth ;
My gentle Phebe did bid me give you this.
I know not the contents ; but, as I guess
By the stern brow and waspish action
Which she did use as she was writing of it,   10
It bears an angry tenour.   Pardon me,
I am but as a guiltless messenger.

ROS. Patience herself would startle at this letter,
And play the swaggerer.   Bear this, bear all.
She says I am not fair, that I lack manners ;   15
She calls me proud, and that she could not love me,
Were man as rare as Phœnix.   'Od's my will !
Her love is not the hare that I do hunt ;
Why writes she so to me ?   Well, shepherd, well,
This is a letter of your own device.   20
SIL. No, I protest, I know not the contents ;
Phebe did write it.
ROS.   Come, come, you are a fool,
And turn'd into the extremity of love.
I saw her hand ; she has a leathern hand,
A freestone-colour'd hand ; I verily did think   25
That her old gloves were on, but 'twas her hands ;
She has a huswife's hand—but that's no matter.
I say she never did invent this letter :
This is a man's invention, and his hand.
SIL. Sure, it is hers.   30
ROS. Why, 'tis a boisterous and a cruel style ;
A style for challengers.   Why, she defies me,
Like Turk to Christian.   Women's gentle brain
Could not drop forth such giant-rude invention,
Such Ethiope words, blacker in their effect   35
Than in their countenance.   Will you hear the letter ?
SIL. So please you, for I never heard it yet ;
Yet heard too much of Phebe's cruelty.
ROS. She Phebes me : mark how the tyrant writes.   [reads.
        ' Art thou god to shepherd turn'd,   40
        That a maiden's heart hath burn'd ? '
Can a woman rail thus ?
SIL. Call you this railing ?
ROS.   ' Why, thy godhead laid apart,
        War'st thou with a woman's heart ? '   45
Did you ever hear such railing ?
        ' Whiles the eye of man did woo me,
        That could do no vengeance to me.'
Meaning me a beast.
        ' If the scorn of your bright eyne   50 | Lines 50–53 omitted.
        Have power to raise such love in mine,
        Alack, in me what strange effect
        Would they work in mild aspect !
        Whiles you chid me, I did love ;
        How then might your prayers move !   55
        He that brings this love to thee
        Little knows this love in me ;
        And by him seal up thy mind,
        Whether that thy youth and kind
        Will the faithful offer take   60
        Of me and all that I can make ;
        Or else by him my love deny,
        And then I'll study how to die.'
SIL. Call you this chiding ?
CEL. Alas, poor shepherd !   65

72

ROS. Do you pity him ? No, he deserves no pity. Wilt thou love
such a woman ? What, to make thee an instrument, and play
false strains upon thee ! Not to be endur'd ! Well, go your way
to her, for I see love hath made thee a tame snake, and say this
to her—that if she love me, I charge her to love thee ; if she will
not, I will never have her unless thou entreat for her. If you
be a true lover, hence, and not a word ; for here comes more
company.   [exit SILVIUS.

Enter OLIVER.

OLI. Good morrow, fair ones ; pray you, if you know,
Where in the purlieus of this forest stands   75
A sheep-cote fenc'd about with olive trees ?
CEL. West of this place, down in the neighbour bottom.
The rank of osiers by the murmuring stream
Left on your right hand brings you to the place.
But at this hour the house doth keep itself ;   80
There's none within.
OLI. If that an eye may profit by a tongue,
Then should I know you by description—
Such garments, and such years : ' The boy is fair,
Of female favour, and bestows himself   85
Like a ripe sister ; the woman low,
And browner than her brother'. Are not you
The owner of the house I did inquire for ?
CEL. It is no boast, being ask'd, to say we are.
OLI. Orlando doth commend him to you both ;   90
And to that youth he calls his Rosalind
He sends this bloody napkin. Are you he ?
ROS. I am. What must we understand by this ?
OLI. Some of my shame ; if you will know of me
What man I am, and how, and why, and where,   95
This handkercher was stain'd.
CEL.   I pray you, tell it.
OLI. When last the young Orlando parted from you,
He left a promise to return again
Within an hour ; and, pacing through the forest,
Chewing the food of sweet and bitter fancy,   100
Lo, what befell ! He threw his eye aside,
And mark what object did present itself.
Under an oak, whose boughs were moss'd with age,
And high top bald with dry antiquity,
A wretched ragged man, o'ergrown with hair,   105
Lay sleeping on his back. About his neck
A green and gilded snake had wreath'd itself,
Who with her head nimble in threats approach'd
The opening of his mouth ; but suddenly,
Seeing Orlando, it unlink'd itself,   110
And with indented glides did slip away
Into a bush ; under which bush's shade
A lioness, with udders all drawn dry.
Lay couching, head on ground, with catlike watch,
When that the sleeping man should stir ; for 'tis   115
The royal disposition of that beast

To prey on nothing that doth seem as dead.
This seen, Orlando did approach the man,
And found it was his brother, his elder brother.   120
CEL. O, I have heard him speak of that same brother ;
And he did render him the most unnatural
That liv'd amongst men.
OLI.   And well he might so do,
For well I know he was unnatural.
ROS. But, to Orlando : did he leave him there,
Food to the suck'd and hungry lioness ?   125
OLI. Twice did he turn his back, and purpos'd so ;
But kindness, nobler ever than revenge,
And nature, stronger than his just occasion,
Made him give battle to the lioness,
Who quickly fell before him ; in which hurtling   130
From miserable slumber I awak'd.
CEL. Are you his brother ?
ROS.   Was't you he rescu'd ?
CEL. Was't you that did so oft contrive to kill him ?
OLI. 'Twas I ; but 'tis not I. I do not shame
To tell you what I was, since my conversion   135
So sweetly tastes, being the thing I am.
ROS. But for the bloody napkin ?
OLI.   By and by.
When from the first to last, betwixt us two,
Tears our recountments had most kindly bath'd,
As how I came into that desert place—   140
In brief, he led me to the gentle Duke,
Who gave me fresh array and entertainment,
Committing me unto my brother's love ;
Who led me instantly unto his cave,
There stripp'd himself, and here upon his arm   145
The lioness had torn some flesh away,
Which all this while had bled ; and now he fainted,
And cried, in fainting, upon Rosalind.
Brief, I recover'd him, bound up his wound,
And, after some small space, being strong at heart,   150
He sent me hither, stranger as I am,
To tell this story, that you might excuse
His broken promise, and to give this napkin,
Dy'd in his blood, unto the shepherd youth   154
That he in sport doth call his Rosalind.   [ROSALIND *swoons.*
CEL. Why, how now, Ganymede . sweet Ganymede !
OLI. Many will swoon when they do look on blood.
CEL. There is more in it. Cousin Ganymede !
OLI. Look, he recovers.
ROS. I would I were at home.
CEL.   We'll lead you thither.   160
I pray you, will you take him by the arm ?
OLI. Be of good cheer, youth. You a man !
You lack a man's heart.
ROS. I do so, I confess it. Ah, sirrah, a body would think this was
well counterfeited. I pray you tell your brother how well I
counterfeited. Heigh-ho !   166

OLI. This was not counterfeit ; there is too great testimony in your complexion that it was a passion of earnest.

ROS. Counterfeit, I assure you.

OLI. Well then, take a good heart and counterfeit to be a man.

ROS. So I do ; but, i' faith, I should have been a woman by right.

CEL. Come, you look paler and paler ; pray you draw homewards. Good sir, go with us.   175

OLI. That will I, for I must bear answer back How you excuse my brother, Rosalind.

ROS. I shall devise something ; but, I pray you, commend my counterfeiting to him. Will you go ?   [*exeunt.*

'That I will . . . counterfeiting to him' omitted.

ACT FIVE.

SCENE I. *The forest.*

Enter TOUCHSTONE *and* AUDREY.

SCENE 25
Exterior. On the banks of a stream in the Forest of Arden. Day.

TOUCH. We shall find a time, Audrey ; patience, gentle Audrey.

AUD. Faith, the priest was good enough, for all the old gentleman's saying.

TOUCH. A most wicked Sir Oliver, Audrey, a most vile Martext. But, Audrey, there is a youth here in the forest lays claim to you.

AUD. Ay, I know who 'tis ; he hath no interest in me in the world ; here comes the man you mean.   9

Enter WILLIAM.

TOUCH. It is meat and drink to me to see a clown. By my troth, we that have good wits have much to answer for ; we shall be flouting ; we cannot hold.   12

WILL. Good ev'n, Audrey.

AUD. God ye good ev'n, William.

WILL. And good ev'n to you, sir.

TOUCH. Good ev'n, gentle friend. Cover thy head, cover thy head ; nay, prithee be cover'd. How old are you, friend ?

WILL. Five and twenty, sir.

TOUCH. A ripe age. Is thy name William ?

WILL. William, sir.   20

TOUCH. A fair name. Wast born i' th' forest here ?

WILL. Ay, sir, I thank God.

TOUCH. ' Thank God.' A good answer. Art rich ?

WILL. Faith, sir, so so.

TOUCH. ' So so ' is good, very good, very excellent good ; and yet it is not ; it is but so so. Art thou wise ?   26

WILL. Ay, sir, I have a pretty wit.

TOUCH. Why, thou say'st well. I do now remember a saying : ' The fool doth think he is wise, but the wise man knows himself to be a fool'. The heathen philosopher, when he had a desire to eat a grape, would open his lips when he put it into his mouth ; meaning thereby that grapes were made to eat and lips to open. You do love this maid ?

'I do now remember . . . lips to open' omitted.

WILL. I do, sir.

TOUCH. Give me your hand. Art thou learned ?   35

WILL. No, sir.

TOUCH. Then learn this of me : to have is to have ; for it is a figure in rhetoric that drink, being pour'd out of a cup into a glass, by filling the one doth empty the other ; for all your writers do consent that ipse is 'he ; now, you are not ipse, for I am he. 41
WILL. Which he, sir ?
TOUCH. He, sir, that must marry this woman. Therefore, you clown, abandon—which is in the vulgar leave—the society—which in the boorish is company—of this female—which in the common is woman—which together is : abandon the society of this female ; or, clown, thou perishest ; or, to thy better understanding, diest ; or, to wit, I kill thee, make thee away, translate thy life into death, thy liberty into bondage. I will deal in poison with thee, or in bastinado, or in steel ; I will bandy with thee in faction : I will o'er-run thee with policy ; I will kill thee a hundred and fifty ways ; therefore tremble and depart. 53
AUD Do, good William.
WILL. God rest you merry, sir. [exit.

Enter CORIN.

COR. Our master and mistress seeks you ; come away. away.
TOUCH. Trip, Audrey, trip, Audrey. I attend, I attend. [exeunt.

SCENE II. *The forest.*

Enter ORLANDO and OLIVER.

ORL. Is't possible that on so little acquaintance you should like her ? that but seeing you should love her ? and loving woo ? and, wooing, she should grant ? and will you persever to enjoy her ?
OLI. Neither call the giddiness of it in question, the poverty of her, the small acquaintance, my sudden wooing, nor her sudden consenting ; but say with me, I love Aliena ; say with her that she loves me ; consent with both that we may enjoy each other. It shall be to your good ; for my father's house and all the revenue that was old Sir Rowland's will I estate upon you, and here live and die a shepherd. 11
ORL. You have my consent. Let your wedding be to-morrow. Thither will I invite the Duke and all's contented followers. Go you and prepare Aliena ; for, look you, here comes my Rosalind.

Enter ROSALIND.

ROS. God save you, brother.
OLI. And you, fair sister. [exit.
ROS. O, my dear Orlando, how it grieves me to see thee wear thy heart in a scarf !
ORL. It is my arm. 20
ROS. I thought thy heart had been wounded with the claws of a lion.
ORL. Wounded it is, but with the eyes of a lady.
ROS. Did your brother tell you how I counterfeited to swoon when he show'd me your handkercher. 25
ORL. Ay, and greater wonders than that.
ROS. O, I know where you are. Nay, 'tis true. There was never any thing so sudden but the fight of two rams and Cæsar's thrasonical brag of ' I came, saw, and overcame '. For your

SCENE 26
Exterior. An Oak Wood in the Forest of Arden. Day.

brother and my sister no sooner met but they look'd ; no sooner look'd but they lov'd ; no sooner lov'd but they sigh'd ; no sooner sigh'd but they ask'd one another the reason ; no sooner knew the reason but they sought the remedy—and in these degrees have they made a pair of stairs to marriage, which they will climb incontinent, or else be incontinent before marriage. They are in the very wrath of love, and they will together. Clubs cannot part them.   38

ORL. They shall be married to-morrow ; and I will bid the Duke to the nuptial. But, O, how bitter a thing it is to look into happiness through another man's eyes ! By so much the more shall I to-morrow be at the height of heart-heaviness, by how much I shall think my brother happy in having what he wishes for.

ROS. Why, then, to-morrow I cannot serve your turn for Rosalind ?

ORL. I can live no longer by thinking.   47

ROS. I will weary you, then, no longer with idle talking. Know of me then—for now I speak to some purpose—that I know you are a gentleman of good conceit. I speak not this that you should bear a good opinion of my knowledge, insomuch I say I know you are ; neither do I labour for a greater esteem than may in some little measure draw a belief from you, to do yourself good, and not to grace me. Believe then, if you please, that I can do strange things. I have, since I was three year old, convers'd with a magician, most profound in his art and yet not damnable. If you do love Rosalind so near the heart as your gesture cries it out, when your brother marries Aliena shall you marry her. I know into what straits of fortune she is driven ; and it is not impossible to me, if it appear not inconvenient to you, to set her before your eyes to-morrow, human as she is, and without any danger.   63

ORL. Speak'st thou in sober meanings ?

ROS. By my life, I do ; which I tender dearly, though I say I am a magician. Therefore put you in your best array, bid your friends ; for if you will be married tomorrow, you shall ; and to Rosalind, if you will.

Enter SILVIUS *and* PHEBE.

Look, here comes a lover of mine, and a lover of hers.

PHE. Youth, you have done me much ungentleness   70
    To show the letter that I writ to you.

ROS. I care not if I have. It is my study
    To seem despiteful and ungentle to you.
    You are there follow'd by a faithful shepherd ;
    Look upon him, love him ; he worships you.   75

PHE. Good shepherd, tell this youth what 'tis to love.

SIL. It is to be all made of sighs and tears ;
    And so am I for Phebe.

PHE. And I for Ganymede.

ORL. And I for Rosalind.

ROS. And I for no woman.   80

SIL. It is to be all made of faith and service ;
    And so am I for Phebe.

PHE. And I for Ganymede.

'for now I speak . . .
if you please, that'
omitted.

77

ORL. And I for Rosalind.   85
ROS. And I for no woman.
SIL. It is to be all made of fantasy,
  All made of passion, and all made of wishes ;
  All adoration, duty, and observance,
  All humbleness, all patience, and impatience,   90
  All purity, all trial, all obedience ;
  And so am I for Phebe.
PHE. And so am I for Ganymede.
ORL. And so am I for Rosalind.
ROS. And so am I for no woman.   95
PHE. If this be so, why blame you me to love you ?
SIL. If this be so, why blame you me to love you ?
ORL. If this be so, why blame you me to love you ?
ROS. Why do you speak too ' Why blame you me to love you ? '
ORL. To her that is not here, nor doth not hear.   101
ROS. Pray you, no more of this ; 'tis like the howling of Irish wolves
  against the moon. [to SILVIUS.] I will help you if I can.
  [to PHEBE.]   I would love you if I could.—Tomorrow meet me
  all together.   [to PHEBE.] I will marry you if ever I marry
  woman, and I'll be married to-morrow.   [to ORLANDO.] I will
  satisfy you if ever I satisfied man, and you shall be married
  to-morrow.   [to SILVIUS.] I will content you if what pleases
  you contents you, and you shall be married to-morrow.   [to
  ORLANDO.] As you love Rosalind, meet.   [to SILVIUS.] As you
  love Phebe, meet ;—and as I love no woman, I'll meet. So, fare
  you well ; I have left you commands.   112
SIL. I'll not fail, if I live.
PHE. Nor I.
ORL. Nor I.   [exeunt.

SCENE III.   The forest.

Enter TOUCHSTONE and AUDREY.

SCENE 27
Exterior. A sheep field
near the Forest of
Arden. Day.

TOUCH. To-morrow is the joyful day, Audrey ; to-morrow will we
  be married.
AUD. I do desire it with all my heart ; and I hope it is no dishonest
  desire to desire to be a woman of the world. Here come two
  of the banish'd Duke's pages.   5

Enter two PAGES.

1 PAGE. Well met, honest gentleman.
TOUCH. By my troth, well met. Come sit, sit, and a song.
2 PAGE. We are for you ; sit i' th' middle.
1 PAGE. Shall we clap into't roundly, without hawking, or spitting,
  or saying we are hoarse, which are the only prologues to a bad
  voice ?   11
2 PAGE. I' faith, i'faith ; and both in a tune, like two gipsies on a horse.

Lines 9–12 omitted.

Song.

It was a lover and his lass,
   With a hey, and a ho, and a hey nonino,   15
That o'er the green corn-field did pass
   In the spring time, the only pretty ring time,

When birds do sing, hey ding a ding, ding.
Sweet lovers love the spring.

Between the acres of the rye,   20
  With a hey, and a ho, and a hey nonino,
These pretty country folks would lie,
  In the spring time, &c.

This carol they began that hour,
  With a hey, and a ho, and a hey nonino,   25
How that a life was but a flower,
  In the spring time, &c.

And therefore take the present time,
  With a hey, and a ho, and a hey nonino,
For love is crowned with the prime,   30
  In the spring time, &c.

TOUCH. Truly, young gentlemen, though there was no great matter in
  the ditty, yet the note was very untuneable.
1 PAGE. You are deceiv'd, sir; we kept time, we lost not our time. 'we kept time' *spoken*
TOUCH. By my troth, yes; I count it but time lost to hear such a *by* 2 PAGE
  foolish song. God buy you; and God mend your voices.
  Come, Audrey.   [*exeunt.*

SCENE IV. *The forest.*

Enter DUKE SENIOR, AMIENS, JAQUES, ORLANDO, OLIVER, *and* CELIA.

DUKE S. Dost thou believe, Orlando, that the boy
  Can do all this that he hath promised?
ORL. I sometimes do believe and sometimes do not:
  As those that fear they hope, and know they fear.

Enter ROSALIND, SILVIUS, *and* PHEBE.

ROS. Patience once more, whiles our compact is urg'd: 5
  You say, if I bring in your Rosalind,
  You will bestow her on Orlando here?
DUKE S. That would I, had I kingdoms to give with her.
ROS. And you say you will have her when I bring her?
ORL. That would I, were I of all kingdoms king.   10
ROS. You say you'll marry me, if I be willing?
PHE. That will I, should I die the hour after.
ROS. But if you do refuse to marry me,
  You'll give yourself to this most faithful shepherd?
PHE. So is the bargain.   15
ROS. You say that you'll have Phebe, if she will?
SIL. Though to have her and death were both one thing.
ROS. I have promis'd to make all this matter even.
  Keep you your word, O Duke, to give your daughter;
  You yours, Orlando, to receive his daughter;   20
  Keep your word, Phebe, that you'll marry me,
  Or else, refusing me, to wed this shepherd;
  Keep your word, Silvius, that you'll marry her
  If she refuse me; and from hence I go,
  To make these doubts all even.   [*exeunt* ROSALIND *and* CELIA.
DUKE S. I do remember in this shepherd boy   26
  Some lively touches of my daughter's favour.

SCENE 28
*Exterior. A large
clearing in the Forest of
Arden. Day.*

ORL. My lord, the first time that I ever saw him
Methought he was a brother to your daughter.
But, my good lord, this boy is forest-born,   30 | Lines 30–34 omitted.
And hath been tutor'd in the rudiments
Of many desperate studies by his uncle,
Whom he reports to be a great magician,
Obscured in the circle of this forest.   34

Enter TOUCHSTONE *and* AUDREY.

JAQ. There is, sure, another flood toward, and these couples are
coming to the ark. Here comes a pair of very strange beasts
which in all tongues are call'd fools.   37
TOUCH. Salutation and greeting to you all!
JAQ. Good my lord, bid him welcome. This is the motley-minded
gentleman that I have so often met in the forest. He hath been
a courtier, he swears.   41
TOUCH. If any man doubt that, let him put me to my purgation.
I have trod a measure ; I have flatt'red a lady ; I have been
politic with my friend, smooth with mine enemy ; I have undone
three tailors ; I have had four quarrels, and like to have fought
one.   46
JAQ. And how was that ta'en up ?
TOUCH. Faith, we met, and found the quarrel was upon the seventh
cause.
JAQ. How seventh cause ? Good my lord, like this fellow.
DUKE S. I like him very well.
TOUCH. God 'ild you, sir ; I desire you of the like. I press in here,
sir, amongst the rest of the country copulatives, to swear and to
forswear, according as marriage binds and blood breaks. A poor
virgin, sir, an ill-favour'd thing, sir, but mine own ; a poor
humour of mine, sir, to take that that no man else will. Rich
honesty dwells like a miser, sir, in a poor house ; as your pearl
in your foul oyster.   59
DUKE S. By my faith, he is very swift and sententious.
| TOUCH. According to the fool's bolt, sir, and such dulcet diseases. | Line 61 omitted.
JAQ. But, for the seventh cause : how did you find the quarrel on
the seventh cause ?   64
TOUCH. Upon a lie seven times removed—bear your body more
seeming, Audrey—as thus, sir. I did dislike the cut of a certain
courtier's beard ; he sent me word, if I said his beard was not
cut well, he was in the mind it was. This is call'd the Retort
Courteous. If I sent him word again it was not well cut, he
would send me word he cut it to please himself. This is call'd
the Quip Modest. If again it was not well cut, he disabled my
judgment. This is call'd the Reply Churlish. If again it was
not well cut, he would answer I spake not true. This is call'd
the Reproof Valiant. If again it was not well cut, he would say
I lie. This is call'd the Countercheck Quarrelsome. And so to
Lie Circumstantial and the Lie Direct.   77
JAQ. And how oft did you say his beard was not well cut ?
TOUCH. I durst go no further than the Lie Circumstantial, nor he
durst not give me the Lie Direct ; and so we measur'd swords
and parted.
| JAQ. Can you nominate in order now the degrees of the lie ?   84 | Lines 84–97 omitted.

TOUCH. O, sir, we quarrel in print by the book, as you have books   Lines 84–97 omitted.
for good manners. I will name you the degrees. The first, the
Retort Courteous ; the second, the Quip Modest ; the third, the
Reply Churlish ; the fourth, the Reproof Valiant ; the fifth, the
Countercheck Quarrelsome ; the sixth, the Lie with Circum-
stance ; the seventh, the Lie Direct. All these you may avoid
but the Lie Direct ; and you may avoid that too with an If.
I knew when seven justices could not take up a quarrel ; but
when the parties were met themselves, one of them thought but
of an If, as : ' If you said so, then 1 said so'. And they shook
hands, and swore brothers. Your If is the only peace-maker ;
much virtue in If.   97
JAQ. Is not this a rare fellow, my lord ?
He's as good at any thing, and yet a fool.
DUKE S. He uses his folly like a stalking-horse, and under the presentation of that he shoots his wit.   101

      Enter HYMEN, ROSALIND, *and* CELIA.   *Still music.*
HYM.   Then is there mirth in heaven,
      When earthly things made even
        Atone together.
      Good Duke, receive thy daughter ;   105
      Hymen from heaven brought her,
        Yea, brought her hither,
      That thou mightst join her hand with his,
      Whose heart within his bosom is.
ROS. [*to* DUKE.]   To you I give myself, for I am yours.   110
  [*to* ORLANDO.]   To you I give myself, for I am yours.
DUKE S.   If there be truth in sight, you are my daughter.
ORL. If there be truth in sight, you are my Rosalind.
PHE. If sight and shape be true,
      Why then, my love adieu !   115
ROS. I'll have no father, if you be not he ;
  I'll have no husband, if you be not he ;
  Nor ne'er wed woman, if you be not she.
HYM.   Peace, ho ! I bar confusion ;
      'Tis I must make conclusion   120
        Of these most strange events.
      Here's eight that must take hands
      To join in Hymen's bands,
        If truth holds true contents.
      You and you no cross shall part ;   125
      You and you are heart in heart ;
      You to his love must accord,
      Or have a woman to your lord ;
      You and you are sure together,
      As the winter to foul weather.   130
      Whiles a wedlock-hymn we sing,
      Feed yourselves with questioning,
      That reason wonder may diminish,
      How thus we met, and these things finish.
          Song.
      Wedding is great Juno's crown ;   135
        O blessed bond of board and bed !   *Sung by* AMIENS.

'Tis Hymen peoples every town ;
  High wedlock then be honoured.
  Honour, high honour, and renown,
    To Hymen, god of every town !   140
DUKE S. O my dear niece, welcome thou art to me !
  Even daughter, welcome in no less degree.
PHE. I will not eat my word, now thou art mine ;
  Thy faith my fancy to thee doth combine.

Enter JAQUES DE BOYS.

JAQ. DE B. Let me have audience for a word or two.   145
  I am the second son of old Sir Rowland,
  That bring these tidings to this fair assembly.
  Duke Frederick, hearing how that every day
  Men of great worth resorted to this forest,
  Address'd a mighty power ; which were on foot,   150
  In his own conduct, purposely to take
  His brother here, and put him to the sword ;
  And to the skirts of this wild wood he came,
  Where, meeting with an old religious man,
  After some question with him, was converted   155
  Both from his enterprise and from the world ;
  His crown bequeathing to his banish'd brother,
  And all their lands restor'd to them again
  That were with him exil'd.   This to be true
  I do engage my life.
DUKE S.   Welcome, young man.   160
  Thou offer'st fairly to thy brothers' wedding :
  To one, his lands withheld ; and to the other,
  A land itself at large, a potent dukedom.
  First, in this forest let us do those ends
  That here were well begun and well begot;   165
  And after, every of this happy number,
  That have endur'd shrewd days and nights with us,
  Shall share the good of our returned fortune,
  According to the measure of their states.
  Meantime, forget this new-fall'n dignity,   170
  And fall into our rustic revelry.
  Play, music ; and you brides and bridegrooms all,
  With measure heap'd in joy, to th' measures fall.
JAQ. Sir, by your patience.   If I heard you rightly,
  The Duke hath put on a religious life,   175
  And thrown into neglect the pompous court.
JAQ DE B. He hath.
JAQ. To him will I.   Out of these convertites
  There is much matter to be heard and learn'd.
  [*to* DUKE.]   You to your former honour I bequeath ;   180
  Your patience and your virtue well deserves it.
  [*to* ORLANDO.]   You to a love that your true faith doth merit ;
  [*to* OLIVER.]   You to your land, and love, and great allies ;
  [*to* SILVIUS.]   You to a long and well-deserved bed ;   184
  [*to* TOUCHSTONE.]   And you to wrangling ; for thy loving voyage
  Is but for two months victuall'd.—So to your pleasures ;
  I am for other than for dancing measures.

DUKE S. Stay, Jaques, stay.
JAQ. To see no pastime I. What you would have
  I'll stay to know at your abandon'd cave.   [*exit.*
DUKE S. Proceed, proceed. We will begin these rites,   191
  As we do trust they'll end, in true delights.   [*a dance. exeunt.*

EPILOGUE.

ROS. It is not the fashion to see the lady the epilogue ; but it is no
more unhandsome than to see the lord the prologue. If it be
true that good wine needs no bush, 'tis true that a good play
needs no epilogue. Yet to good wine they do use good bushes ;
and good plays prove the better by the help of good epilogues.
What a case am I in then, that am neither a good epilogue, nor
cannot insinuate with you in the behalf of a good play ! I am
not furnish'd like a beggar ; therefore to beg will not become
me. My way is to conjure you ; and I'll begin with the women.
I charge you, O women, for the love you bear to men, to like as
much of this play as please you ; and I charge you, O men, for
the love you bear to women—as I perceive by your simp'ring
none of you hates them—that between you and the women the
play may please. If I were a woman, I would kiss as many of
you as had beards that pleas'd me, complexions that lik'd me,
and breaths that I defied not ; and, I am sure, as many as have
good beards, or good faces, or sweet breaths, will, for my kind
offer, when I make curtsy, bid me farewell.

GLOSSARY

Graham S. May

Difficult phrases are listed under the most important or most difficult word in them. If no such word stands out, they are listed under the first word.

Words appear in the form they take in the text. If they occur in several forms, they are listed under the root form (singular for nouns, infinitive for verbs).

Line references are given only when the same word is used with different meanings, and when there are puns.

ABUSE, (i) misuse (III ii 334); (ii) deceive (III v 78, IV i 192)
ACCOUTREMENTS, clothing
ACRES, areas of tilled land
ADDRESS'D, gathered, prepared
ADVENTURE, hazardous enterprise; 'hard adventure', chance painful and unlucky experience
AFTER, for (III v 45); 'after kind', act according to her nature (with innuendo)
AGAIN, often = 'back again'
AGAINST, anticipating (IV i 134)
ALIENA, i.e. 'she who is not herself'
ALLOTTERY, allocated share
ALLOWS YOU, acknowledges you to be
ALONG, at full length (II i 30, III ii 224)
AMAZE, bewilder
AN, if
AN IF, if
ANATOMIZE, dissect, expose the (moral) nature of
ANON, immediately
ANSWER YOU, retort, assert in exchange that you are
APART, aside; 'laid apart', set aside temporarily
ARGUMENT, (i) reason (I ii 258); (ii) subject (III i 3)
ARMED IN HIS FORTUNE, already equipped with his cuckold's horns
ARRAY, clothing
AS, such as (IV iii 140)
ASPECT, (i) look, expression; (ii) (in astrology) relative position, and hence 'influence', of a heavenly body

ASSAYED, attempted
AT LARGE, 'A land itself at large', a whole kingdom
ATALANTA'S BETTER PART, her chastity, rather than her cupidity and cruelty to her suitors. She was of great nimbleness, and refused to marry unless her suitor could outrun her. Melanion eventually won her hand by dropping golden apples in her path, which delayed her as she bent to retrieve them. 'Made of Atalanta's heels', constructed out of the swiftest material
ATHWART, ineptly awry across (rather than cleanly piercing)
ATOMIES, tiny particles
ATONE, are reconciled, joined as one
ATTEMPT, enterprise
ATTEND, follow, am coming (V i 57)
ATTORNEY, proxy
AVOID, evade (V iv 90)

BAG AND BAGGAGE, phrase used of an honourably retreating army, which, as it still carries with it all its equipment, is clearly undefeated
BANDS, 'Hymen's bands', (i) the bonds of wedlock; (ii) the ranks of those who are married
BANDY, contend
BANQUET, light meal of wine and fruit
BAR, prohibit
BARBARY COCK-PIGEON, male dove of a type introduced from Asia (Barbary), noted for its jealousy
BASTARD OF VENUS, Cupid, the blind son

84

of Venus by Mercury, rather than by her husband Vulcan

BASTINADO, beating with a cudgel

BATLER, wooden club used for beating clothes when washing them

BAWDRY, sin, unchastity

BEAR, sing (IV ii 11 stage-direction)

BECOME, suit, befit; 'becomes the ground', suits the earth, befits the background

BEGGARLY, excessive, fulsome, such as could be expected from a beggar

BEGOT, commenced (V iv 165)

BEHOLDING, under an obligation

BELLS, 'the falcon her bells', allusion to the bells tied to a falcon to tame her

BELL-WETHER, leader of the flock

BERHYM'D, celebrated in and afflicted by verses

BESTOWS HIMSELF LIKE, carried himself like, has the manner of

BETTER PART MADE MERCY, created for the better part merciful by disposition

BILL, caress beak with beak

BILLS, (i) hedging-tools; (ii) labels; (iii) legal documents (pun, I ii 107)

BLOOD, (rights of) blood-relationship; 'in the gentle condition of blood', according to the honourable obligations conferred by kinship; 'diverted blood', perversion of the natural blood-relationship; 'blood breaks', appetite demands

BLUE EYE, eye ringed with dark shadows of sleeplessness

BOARD, daily provisions

BOB, scoff, jest at someone's expense

BODY, 'a body', a person, anyone

BONNY, robust, sturdy

BOORISH, rustic (parlance)

BOTTOM, valley, hollow (IV iii 77)

BOUNDEN, indebted

BOUNDS, lands; 'bounds of feed', full extent of pastures

BOW, yoke (III iii 69)

BRANCH OF VICTORY, crown to denote success (like the palm-crown given to a victorious Roman military leader)

BRAVE, fine

BRAVERY, fine, ostentatious clothes

BREATH'D, exercised, warmed up

BREATHER, living being

BRIEF, in brief (IV iii 149)

BRING ME OUT, put me out

BROKEN MUSIC, music divided into separate parts for several instruments

BROOK (v.), endure

BROWNER, with browner hair

BUGLE, black glass bead

BURDEN, refrain, chorus, or perhaps 'bass part sung in harmony' (III ii 232, IV ii 11)

BURGHERS, citizens

BURS, prickly flower-heads which catch and cling to clothing

BUSH, 'needs no bush', needs no advertisement (green branches were hung outside wine-merchants' shops to identify them)

BUT, (i) only; (ii) except; (iii) unless (III iii 44); (iv) without he (III v 6); 'but poor a', merely; 'not in the mind but', I am inclined to think that; 'but one cast away', only one woman cast off

BUTCHERY, slaughter-house

BUTTER-WOMEN'S RANK TO MARKET, movement of butter-women riding in a heavy jog-trot to market, one after the other

BY THE WAY, on the way

CAESAR'S THRASONICAL BRAG, Julius Caesar's boastful claim (made about the ease of his final victory in his Pontic campaign)

CAGE OF RUSHES, reed-built (i.e. very flimsy) prison

CALL FOOLS INTO A CIRCLE, incite fools to huddle together much as a magician confines dangerous spirits within a defined area

CALL ME NOT A FOOL TILL HEAVEN HATH SENT ME FORTUNE, allusion to the proverb 'fortunè favours fools'

CALLING, (i) name; (ii) station in life; (iii) vocation (III iii 94)

CANDLE, 'with candle', diligently (allusion to Luke xv 8); 'I see no more in you Than without candle may go dark to bed . . .', as far as I am concerned, you are quite ordinary: if you had no candle, you would go to bed in darkness just like anyone else. (Perhaps an allusion to the proverb 'The Heathen, when they died, went to bed without a candle', i.e. you are no more than a mere heathen)

CAPABLE IMPRESSURE, (i) impression that can be received; (ii) imprint that can retain the initial impression

CAPARISON'D, (of a horse) covered with a cloth, harnessed, decked; here, 'dressed'

CAPERS, unexpected, freakish behaviour

CAPON, chicken bred for the table (notoriously used as a bribe to influence justices)

CAPRICIOUS, (i) whimsical, wayward, temperamental; (ii) goat-like, lascivious

CARELESS, (i) carefree (II i 52); (ii) beyond caring (III ii 352)

CARLOT, peasant

CART, 'to cart', (i) loaded on to a cart like harvested corn; (ii) given the punishment, meted out to prostitutes, of public exposure on a cart

CASE, predicament

CAST LIPS, (i) lips cast off, thrown away; (ii) lips produced in a mould taken from the original, i.e. 'authentic'

CHANTICLEER, traditional name for a loquacious cock

CHARACTER, inscribe

CHASE, chain of argument (I iii 30)

CHECK, taunt, rebuff

CHEERLY, cheerful (II vi 11); be cheerful, take comfort (II vi 14)

CHOKE THEIR SERVICE UP, stifle their willingness to serve

CHOPT, chapped

CICATRICE, scar; scar-like mark

CIPHER, a figure nought, zero

CIRCUMSTANTIAL, indirect or conditional

CIVET, perfume made from the 'flux' or glandular secretion of the civet cat

CIVIL SAYINGS, serious maxims

CLAP INTO'T ROUNDLY, begin promptly, without unnecessary fuss, and with gusto

CLAPP'D HIM O'TH'SHOULDER, (i) attracted his attention with a tap on the shoulder; (ii) encourage him with a slap (i.e. he is not very much in love); (iii) arrested him (i.e. he is deeply in love)

CLEAR ALL, solve all the problems

CLEOPATRA, Queen of Egypt, mistress of Julius Caesar and Mark Antony, renowned for intelligence, beauty and charm

CLOWN, (i) yokel, country bumpkin; (ii) fool or jester (II ii 8)

CLUBS, (i) cudgels; (ii) the cry ('Clubs') customarily made to summon help to break up a street brawl

COD, husk of a pea-pod

COLOUR, type, kind (I ii 90, III ii 378)

COME OFF, escape

COME YOUR WAYS, come on, begin

COMFORT, take comfort (II vi 4)

COMFORTABLE, comforted

COMMISSION, authority

COMPACT, contract

COMPACT OF JARS, composed of discords

COMPANY, 'last company', joining us just now

COMPLAIN'D OF, uttered a lament about

CONCEIT, imagination; 'of good conceit', intelligent

CONCEIVE, imagine

CONDITION, mood (I ii 243); 'in the gentle condition of blood', according to the honourable obligations conferred by kinship

CONDUCT, 'In his own conduct', under his personal leadership

CONEY, rabbit

CONFINES, boundaries, territories

CONJURE, cast spells upon

CONNED THEM OUT OF RINGS, learned them by heart from the commonplace sentiments often engraved upon rings

CONSENT, agree (V i 39)

CONTENTS, 'If truth hold true contents', if the state of affairs now revealed (by the removal of the disguise) is such that it would indeed ensure real happiness

CONTRIVE, scheme

CONVERS'D, (i) associated; (ii) studied

CONVERTITES, those who abandon loose living for a virtuous life

COPE, encounter; debate with

COPULATIVES, those about to be coupled or married

COST, expensive apparel; 'on my cost', bought at my expense, i.e. any business of mine

COTE, cottage

COUCHING, lying in ambush, lurking

COUNTENANCE, (i) demeanour; (ii) appearance (IV i 32; IV iii 36)

COUNTER, worthless imitation coin

COUPLE, marry

COUPLED, as close together as a pair of hounds leashed together (I iii 72)

COURS'D, chased, raced

COURTESY OF NATIONS, conventions of the civilised world

COURTSHIP, (i) courtly manners; (ii) wooing (pun)

COUSIN, term used of all close kindred (IV iii 157)

COVER THE WHILE, lay the table meanwhile

COVER'D, 'be cover'd', replace your hat

COVERED GOBLET, the body and domed lid of a goblet formed a hollow sphere

COZ, 'cousin', used indiscriminately for close kindred

CREST, heraldic sign on a helmet to distinguish the wearer

CROSS, (i) affliction (V iv 125); (ii) silver coin (pun at II iv 10 on (i), (ii), and perhaps

Matthew x 38, 'And he that doth not take his cross and follow after me, is not worthy of me')

CURB, chain or strap for checking an unruly horse

CURS, dogs

CURTLE-AXE, short sword

CURVET, leap about, frolic

DAMASK, (i) rich, patterned Damascus silk; (ii) a type of pale red rose

DAMNABLE, 'not damnable', not liable to be punished with damnation (as he does not practise black magic)

DARK HOUSE AND A WHIP, imprisonment in darkness and whipping was the standard Elizabethan treatment for the insane

DEAD SHEPHERD, Christopher Marlowe: an allusion to his poem *Hero and Leander*, I, 176

DEARLY, (i) expensively (I i 10); (ii) intensely (I iii 31)

DEFENCE, the ability to defend oneself

DEFIED NOT, took no objection to

DEGREES, steps (with pun on 'stairs')

DESIRE, 'I desire you of the like', I hope you do like me, or, I beg to return the compliment

DESOLATION, despondency

DESPERATE, dangerous

DESPITE, 'in despite of my invention', in spite of my (lack of) creative imagination

DESPITEFUL, contemptuous

DETECT, expose

DEVICE, (i) thoughts (I i 47); (ii) devising (IV iii 20)

DIAL, watch, or pocket sun-dial

DIANA, goddess of virginity and hunting; 'Diana in the fountain', perhaps (i) an allusion to the heroine of Montemayor's *Diana*, who spends much of her time weeping; or (ii) an allusion to an actual fountain adorned with a statue of the goddess

DIFFERENCE (II i 6), (i) change; (ii) strife, dissension

DISABLE, belittle, disparage

DISCOVERING, revealing

DISHONEST, unchaste

DISLIKE, express an aversion to

DISPATCH, (i) deal with quickly; (ii) put to death

DISPOSITION, mental outlook (III ii 182)

DISPUTABLE, argumentative

DISSEMBLING COLOUR, red, as Judas's hair was traditionally portrayed

DO, 'what had he to do', what business was it of his

DO HIM RIGHT, describes him justly

DOG-APES, baboons

DOLE, lamentation

DOOM, judgement, sentence

DOUBLET AND HOSE, jacket and trousers (distinctively male garments)

DRAVE, drove

DRY, in contemporary physiology a dry brain was thought to be slow to take in an impression, but sure to retain it (II vii 39)

DUCDAME, perhaps (i) garbled Latin ('Lead him to me'); (ii) Welsh ('Come to me'); (iii) Italian ('Take him away'). Probably, however, deliberately obscure, 'Greek', i.e. gibberish

DULCET DISEASES, sweet weakness, i.e. witty gibes

EARNEST, 'of earnest', genuine

EDUCATION, the poor education he gives me

EFFECT, purport, meaning (IV iii 35)

EFFIGIES, likeness

EMBOSSED, swollen, purulent, protuberant

EMULATION, a consequence upon professional jealousy

EMULATOR, one who jealously strives to rival

ENCHANTINGLY, as if he bewitched them

ENDS, 'do those ends', achieve those aims

ENGAGE, pledge

ENJOY, wed

ENTAME, tame

ENTERTAIN, receive kindly

ENTERTAINMENT, hospitality (food, accommodation) fit for a guest

ENVENOMS, (i) poisons; (ii) makes him to be treated by others as if he were dangerous or poisonous

ENVIOUS, given to enmity or hatred (II i 4)

EREWHILE, a short time ago

ERRING, wandering

ERST, not long ago

ESTATE (n.), predicament; (v.) legally bestow

ETHIOPE, Ethiopian, i.e. black

EVEN (adj.), unravelled, set to rights (V iv 18, V iv 25); harmoniously equal (V iv 103); (adv.), just, only (III iii 66); 'even daughter', either (i) (to Celia) 'no less than a daughter', or (ii) (to Rosalind) 'and you, my true daughter'; (n.), evening (II iv 64, III iii 63)

EVERY, each (V iv 166)

EXCUSE, judge leniently

EXERCISES, occupations

EXPEDIENTLY, in haste
EXTENT, writ for initiating the legal seizure of land
EXTERMIN'D, destroyed, ended
EYNE, eyes

FACTION, strife, dissension
FAIN, be glad to (I ii 142); wish to (III iii 40); obliged (IV i 53)
FAIR (adj.), healthy (I i 9)
FAITH, fidelity; indeed (III v 45)
FALL (n.), tumble in wrestling (innuendo)
FALLS, drops
FALSE GALLOP, canter
FANCY, love, amorous desire; love thoughts (IV iii 100)
FANCY-MONGER one who trades in love
FANTASTICAL, capricious, whimsical
FANTASY, imagination ungoverned by reason; amorous desire
FASHION, 'for fashion sake', for form's or appearances' sake
FAVOUR, complexion, countenance, appearance
FEATURE, form
FEEDER, shepherd
FEELINGLY, (i) by making themselves felt; (ii) vividly; (iii) sympathetically
FEET, units of rhythm in verse (pun, III ii 156)
FEIGN, (i) pretend, tell untruths; (ii) relate fictionally, write from the imagination (puns on (i), (ii), and perhaps on 'fain'='desire', III iii 16ff)
FELLS, fleeces
FIGURE, (i) form, image (III ii 272); (ii) stylistic device (V i 36)
FIND, find your way out of (V iv 63)
FLEET THE TIME CARELESSLY, make time pass swiftly in a carefree manner
FLOUT, mock; 'shall be flouting', must jeer
FLUX, (i) liquid flow (II i 52); (ii) glandular secretion (III ii 60)
FOIL, (i) defeat; (ii) throw (in wrestling)
FOND TO, foolish as to
FOOL, (i) jester; (ii) simple creature (II i 22, II i 40)
FOOL'S BOLT, allusion to the proverb 'A fool's bolt (or arrow) is soon shot'
FOR, (i) because of (I iii 9); (ii) possessed of (III ii 376); what about (IV iii 137)
FORKED HEADS, barbed arrows
FORSOOTH, in truth, indeed
FORWARD, eager, precocious (III iii 10)
FORWARDNESS, rashness

FOUL, 'I thank the gods I am foul', I can't help being ugly, I was born that way; 'Foul is most foul, being foul to be a scoffer', ugliness is made yet more ugly, when to it is added the moral disfigurement of ill-nature
FRANTIC, out of one's senses
FREE, guiltless (II vii 85)
FREESTONE-COLOURED, the colour of greyish-yellow sandstone
FRIENDLY, as a friend
FRIENDS, relatives
FULL, whole (III ii 4)
FURNISH'D, dressed, equipped

GAMESTER, (i) athlete; (ii) sprightly young man
GANYMEDE, a beautiful youth, the cup-bearer, of Zeus
GARGANTUA'S MOUTH, a mouth the size of a fairy-tale giant, or the giant of a story by Rabelais
GENERAL CHALLENGER, one who will take on all comers
GENTILITY, honourable birth
GENTLE, well-born, honourable, courteous
GESTURE, demeanour
GIANT RUDE, hugely barbarous, of giant-like ungainliness
GIDDINESS, rashness
GIDDY, stupid, frivolous
GILDED, covered with a golden hue
GIPSIES, 'two gipsies on a horse', two gipsies sitting one behind the other on a horse, singing together
GIVE THE LIE TO THEIR CONSCIENCES, accuse their consciences to their face of lying
GLANCES, innuendoes, satirical hits
GLEAN, gather (scarce quantities)
GO ALONE, walk without a crutch
GO TO, exclamation of mild impatience, i.e. 'get away'
GO YOUR WAYS, go away
GOD BUY YOU, God be with you, i.e. 'good-bye'
GOD YE, God give you
GODDILD YOU, God yield (i.e. reward) you
GOES BEFORE, anticipates
GOLDEN WORLD, allusion to the Golden Age, a legendary epoch of pastoral peace and happiness
GOOD FAITH, in truth
GOOD LEAVE, willing permission
GOOD MY COMPLEXION!, as I hope my whole temperament may be good!

GOODS, 'Many a man knows no end of his goods', many are materially very well-off

GRACE, pity, sympathy (III v 99)

GRACE HIMSELF ON THEE, gain honour for himself at your expense

GRACE ME, add to my reputation

GRACIOUS, lucky, fortunate, in favour

GRAFF, graft

GRAVELL'D, run aground, perplexed, at a loss

GROSS, (i) whole; (ii) large (IV i 174)

GROUND, (i) earth; (ii) background of a picture (pun, III ii 225)

GROW UPON, (i) grow up; (ii) take liberties with

HABIT, 'under that habit', either (i) according to that customary mode of behaviour; or (ii) beneath that disguise

HAND, handwriting (IV iii 29)

HANDKERCHER, handkerchief

HARD, vigorous (III ii 297); 'trots hard', moves at an uncomfortable jog-trot

HARD MATTER, 'it is a hard matter for friends to meet . . .', it's hard for friends to meet, but not impossible, for even mountains can meet each other, when moved by earthquakes. (Allusion to proverb 'Friends may meet, but mountains never greet')

HARD-FAVOURED, ugly

HARM, misfortunes

HART, stag

HAVE TO PAY FOR IT OF US, we will give you the money to pay for it

HAVE WITH YOU, I am coming with you

HAVING IN BEARD, amount of beard you possess

HAWKING, clearing the throat

HEADED EVILS, evils (or 'skin-sores') that have grown to a head (formed a protuberance like that of a boil)

HEART, pun on 'hart' = stag (III ii 231)

HELEN, Helen of Troy, wife of Menelaus, whose abduction by Paris led to the Trojan War. Symbol of female beauty, but also criticised for wantonness

HEM, (i) sew a border; (ii) cough; (pun, I iii 17; pun on sounds of 'hem' and 'him', I iii 19)

HERCULES, classical hero, considered to be the ideal of physical strength

HIND, (i) farm-servant (I i 15); (ii) female deer (III ii 91)

HISTORY, chronicle play

HOLD, refrain (V i 12)

HOLD INTELLIGENCE, communicate, i.e. understand

HOLIDAY, festive

HOLLA, whoa! (cry to check a horse)

HOMILY OF LOVE, religious discourse on love delivered to a congregation

HONEST, chaste

HONESTY, virtue, chastity

HONOUR, 'jealous in honour', quick to take offence in matters thought to concern his honour

HOPE, indulge only in vain wishful thinking (V iv 4)

HORNS, husbands, once cuckolded, were said to grow horns on their foreheads, as a sign of their shame

HORN-BEASTS, (i) horned animals; (ii) cuckolds (see HORNS) (pun)

HOSE, breeches

HOUSE, family (I ii 207)

HOW, whether, to what extent (IV ii 8)

HOW NOW WIT, see WIT, WHITHER WILT

HUMAN AS SHE IS, in the flesh

HUMOROUS, moody, temperamental, whimsical

HUMOUR, temperamental mood, whim; 'from his mad humour of love to a living humour of madness', from his merely foolish affectation of love to a thorough and authentic condition of insanity

HUNTRESS, follower of Diana, goddess of the hunt, i.e. Rosalind

HURTLING, tumult, violent conflict

HUSWIFE'S, housewife's

HYEN, hyena

HYMEN, god of marriage

'ILD, reward

ILL-FAVOUR'D, ugly

ILL-FAVOUREDLY, in an ugly fashion (I ii 35); badly, or with a disapproving expression (III ii 246)

IMPRESSURE, impression, imprint

IN HAND, being dealt with

IN LITTLE, in miniature, contracted into a small space

IN PRINT, (i) in a precise way; (ii) according to a contemporary textbook upon the art of quarrelling

IN WINE, in one's cups, when drunk

INCISION, (i) blood-letting to cure mental sickness; (ii) scoring of meat for roasting; (iii) grafting to improve a wild plant

INCONTINENT, (i) immediately; (ii) unchaste; (pun V ii 35)
INCONVENIENT, inappropriate (i.e. wrong for me to be practising magic)
INDE, Indies
INDENTED, zigzagging, undulating
INLAND, city, i.e. well brought up, cultured; 'inland bred', bred close to civilisation, well bred, cultured
INSINUATE WITH, subtly persuade
INSOMUCH, in as much as
INSTANCE, (give an) example; 'modern instances', trite examples
INTENDMENT, intention
INTEREST IN, claim upon, legal title to
INVECTIVELY, vehemently, vituperatively
INVENTION, (lack of) creative imagination (II v 42)
IPSE, 'he himself' (Latin)
IRISH RAT, a rat which the Irish were said to believe could be killed by the incantation of a rhyming spell
IRISH WOLVES dogs howling at the moon were proverbially the image of futile clamour
I'TH'SUN, freely, in the open air

JOVE IN A THATCH'D HOUSE, the supreme classical deity Jupiter in a dwelling completely unsuited to his rank. Allusion to Ovid's tale (*Metamorphoses* VIII, 626ff) of the hospitality offered by the poor Baucis and Philemon to the disguised Jupiter and Mercury, when everyone else had refused them shelter
JUNO'S CROWN, the crown of Juno, wife of Jupiter, and patroness of marriage and married women
JUNO'S SWANS, the swans which drew Venus' chariot, and which belonged to Juno, queen of the gods
JUST, precisely, exactly so (III ii 249)
JUSTLY, precisely

KILL THEM UP, totally slaughter
KIND, (i) respect (II i 27); (ii) species of creature (II vii 90); (iii) nature (IV iii 59); 'after kind', act according to her nature (with innuendo)
KINDLED, born (of rabbits)
KINDLY, IV iii 139, (i) sympathetically; (ii) in true kinship
KINDNESS, (i) kinship; (ii) generosity
KNAVE, 'play the knave', act the role of rogue, trickster

KNOLL'D, rung (in summons)
KNOW, acknowledge (I i 41)

LADY FORTUNE, fortune was often personified as a goddess
LAID APART, (temporarily) set aside
LAID TO THE CHARGE OF, accused
LEAN, 'lean and wasteful', causing one to waste away (from overwork)
LEANDER, youth who swam the Hellespont to visit his mistress, Hero, every night until he was drowned
LEATHERN, leather-like
LEARN, teach (I ii 4)
LEER, (i) complexion; (ii) brownish cattle-colour (i.e. 'of a better leer' = not so sunburnt); (iii) flank or loin
LEFT, passed (IV iii 79)
LIE, accusation of lying
LIEF, 'I had as lief', I would wish just as much (I i 129, IV i 46); I would have liked just as much to (III ii 238)
LIEGE, lord
LIES, 'in him lies', is in his ability
LIEU, 'In lieu of', in return for
LIGHT UPON, chance upon
LIK'D, pleased
LIKE, (i) likely (III iii 79, IV i 62); (ii) almost (V iv 45)
LIMN'D, painted, portrayed
LIN'D, (i) delineated, drawn (III ii 82); (ii) mounted, covered (of a bitch); (iii) given a warm lining; (pun on (ii) and (iii), III ii 95)
LINEAMENTS, facial features
LISP, affect a foreign accent
LIVELY, lifelike
LIVER, organ which was believed to be the seat of the passions
LOOK YOU, (i) be sure you (I iii 121); (ii) seek you (II v 28)
LOVE-PRATE, chattering about love
LOVING VOYAGE, journey of matrimony
LOW, (i) short; (ii) humble (II iii 68)
LUCRETIA, Roman woman who committed suicide after being violated by Tarquin, the subject of Shakespeare's poem *Lucrece*
LUSTY, (i) vigorous; (ii) associated with sexual desire (IV ii 17)

MAKE, (i) create; (ii) do; (pun on (i) and (ii), I i 26ff); (iii) shut (IV i 144); (iv) do or bring with me (IV iii 61); 'What make you here?', what are you doing here?
MANAGE, training, 'paces', of a horse

MARK, notice, take note; 'marked of', observed by

MARKETS, 'you are not for all markets', you are not attractive enough to be sure of more than a few opportunities for marriage

MARRY, to be sure

MASTER WHAT-YE-CALL'T, Mr Latrine, Privy (pun on Jaques = Jakes, slang for latrine)

MATERIAL, (i) full of 'matter', significant notions; or (ii) practical, unromantic

MATTER, significant ideas; 'no matter', by the way, of no importance; 'though there was no great matter in the ditty', although the song is perhaps too insignificant to justify such quibbling

MEANS, gainful employment (III ii 23)

MEASURE, stately formal dance; 'with measure', liberally

MEASURED SWORDS, measured the length of the swords as a preliminary to the duel, to ensure no unfair advantage

MEDLAR, tree whose fruit is edible only when decayed (pun on 'meddler', he who interferes)

MEED, reward

MELANCHOLY, dark, shadowy (II vii 111)

MEMORY, memorial

MEND, improve

MERCY, 'cry the man mercy', beg the man's forgiveness

MERE, complete, utter, nothing but

MERELY, completely, utterly

MESSENGER, (i) message-bearer; (ii) arresting-officer; (pun)

METTLE, substance, spirit

MEWLING, mewing like a cat

MIGHT, 'of might', to have much force or truth

MIND, opinion

MINES, undermines

MINGLED DAMASK, the blended colours of (i) the damask rose, (ii) Damascus silk

MISPRISED, despised, underrated

MODERN, trite, commonplace

MONSTROUS, abnormal

MOONISH, changeable

MORAL, (i) (v.) moralise; (ii) (adj.) moralistic

MORALIZE, draw morals from

MORE IN IT, more to it than just that

MORTAL, (i) subject to death; (ii) extreme (pun, II iv 49–50)

MOTLEY, the fool's distinctive long child's coat, i.e. 'you proper, genuine, fool', (III iii 68); 'motley fool', authentically foolish fool; 'Motley's the only wear', the fool's dress is all the fashion

MOTLEY-MINDED, foolish

MYSELF ALONE, on my own

NAME, reputation (I iii 76)

NAPKIN, handkerchief

NATURAL, (adj.), 'natural brother', blood-brother; 'natural philosopher', (i) philosopher who studies nature; (ii) foolish pretender to thought (pun); (n.), an idiot by birth (I ii 44, I ii 49)

NECESSARY, inevitable

NEEDLESS, which did not need it

NEIGHBOURLY, allusion to the biblical injunction that one should love one's neighbour as oneself

NEW-FANGLED, fond of, and easily distracted by, novelty

NICE, (affectedly) fastidious, refined

NOTE, melody

NOUGHT, bad, worthless; 'be nought awhile', keep quiet, make yourself scarce for a while'

NURTURE, culture, manners

OBSCURED, concealed

OBSERVANCE, attention (III ii 218); respect, humble attention (V ii 89)

OBSERVATION, observed truth or fact; rule or maxim gathered from experience

OCCASION, 'take occasion', take the opportunity; 'her husband's occasion', the opportunity of finding fault in her husband; 'just occasion', legitimate excuse, or perfect opportunity

ODDS, superiority

'ODS, may God save; ''Ods my will', as God is my will

OF, (i) modern uses; (ii) often 'by'; (iii) for (III i 4); (iv) from (III ii 141)

OFFER, propose

OFFER'ST FAIRLY, bring a handsome wedding present

OFTEN RUMINATION, frequent meditation

OMITTANCE IS NO QUITTANCE, failure to do something at the time does not remove one's duty to do it in the long run

ON, as a condition of obtaining (I i 3)

ONE, 'all one', of no importance; 'but one cast away', only one woman cast off

ONLY, habitual, customary

OR, either

91

ORCHARD, probably 'garden'

ORDINARY (adj.), common, widespread; (n.), ordinary stock, ordinary run

OUT, (i) at a loss (IV i 67, IV i 72); (ii) blind (IV i 193); be off! (III ii 89); 'out of', i.e. reflected in (III v 55); 'out of all whooping', beyond all that cries of wonder can express; 'bring me out', throw me off my stride, make me lose my thread

OUT OF SUITS WITH, no longer in favour with

OVID, Roman poet (c. 43BC–AD17), author of the *Ars Amatoria* (*The Art of Love*), notorious for being 'capricious' (=licentious) and far from 'honest' (=chaste). He was exiled from Rome and forced to live along the Goths (pronounced 'goats')

OWE, 'they owe me nothing', i.e. I don't need their signatures ('names') on legal documents because they don't owe me anything

PAINTED CLOTH, cloth painted with moralistic pictures and inscriptions as a cheap substitute for tapestry

PAIR OF STAIRS, flight of stairs

PALE, overcast (I iii 100)

PANCAKES, meat fritters

PANEL, (i) section of a wainscot; (ii) harlot; (pun)

PANTALOON, the stock Doting Old Man of Italian comedy

PARCELS, 'In parcels', piece by piece, feature by feature

PARD, panther or leopard

PARLOUS, perilous

PART, depart from (II i 51)

PARTS, qualities, abilities, talents; roles (III vii 142)

PARTY, person

PASSING SHORT, extremely curt

PASSION OF EARNEST, genuine emotion

PATHETICAL, miserable, annoying, shocking

PEASCOD, pea-pod

PEEVISH, silly

PENALTY OF ADAM, the transformation of the perpetual summer of Eden into the wearying cycle of the seasons, as a punishment for the Fall from God's grace

PERFORCE, forcibly

PERIL, 'his own peril on his forwardness', on his own head be the consequences of his rashness

PERPEND, weigh the facts

PERSON, 'in her person', in my assumed role of Rosalind; 'in mine own person', speaking for myself

PHEBES ME, addresses me in her own style

PHOENIX, mythical Arabian bird, only one of which could be alive at any one time

PHYSIC (n.), medicine; (v.) cure

PICK-PURSE, pickpocket

PLACE, safe home (II iii 27)

PLACES, (i) commonplaces, stock topics or lines of thought which served as foundations for discourse; (ii) compartments for storage; (pun)

PLEASE, may please (Epilogue 11)

PLY, work upon, urge

POINT-DEVICE, neat and trim

POKE, pocket, wallet, large bag, or even the fool's motley coat itself

POLICY, stratagems

POLITIC, crafty, calculated, motivated by expediency

POMPOUS, full of pomp, resplendent

POVERTY, 'And I in such a poverty of grace', and so little pity or sympathy has been shown to me

PRACTICES, plots

PRACTISE, plot

PRESENTATION, (i) theatrical show; (ii) mere pretence

PRESENTLY, immediately

PRESENTS, present legal documents (allusion to characteristic opening phrases of such documents, and pun on 'presence' = demeanour)

PREVENTS, anticipates, forestalls

PRIME, 'with the prime', (i) in spring time; (ii) with perfection

PRITHEE, beg you

PRIVATE, secluded, not public

PRIZER, prize-fighter

PROFESS, (i) affirm the efficacy of; (ii) make my profession; (iii) declare myself expert in

PROFIT, progress

PROPER, (i) well-formed, handsome; (ii) correct (III ii 288)

PROPERER, more handsome

PROVE, turn out to be (IV i 163)

PROVIDE, provide for, make preparation for

PUBLIC HAUNT, general frequentation by men

PULPITER, preacher

PUNY, inferior, petty

PURCHASE, acquire

PURGATION, (i) medical purging; (ii) in theology, the clearing of the soul from guilt;

(iii) in law, proving of innocence, particularly by ordeal; 'put me to my purgation', put me to the test

PURLIEUS, tracts of land on the border of a forest

PURPOS'D SO, intended to do so

PUT, force (I ii 85, IV i 71)

PYTHAGORAS, Greek philosopher (flourished c. 540–510 BC) who believed in the transmigration of souls

QUAIL, slacken, shrink back

QUEEN OF NIGHT, see THRICE-CROWNED QUEEN OF NIGHT

QUESTION, conversation, discussion (III iv 31, V iv 155)

QUINTAIN, wooden post at which riders aimed their lances when practising tilting

QUIT, acquit

QUOTIDIAN, daily recurrent fever

RAGGED, hoarse

RAIL, utter abuse; 'rail against the first-born of Egypt', allusion to Exodus xii 29–30, which tells of the night of the passover, in which the Lord 'smote all the firstborn in the land of Egypt', in reaction to which the Egyptians raised 'a great cry'

RANG'D, wandered at large

RANK, (i) normal status and nature; (ii) evil smell; (pun, I ii 95–96); row (IV iii 78)

RANKER, more suspect, in a worse condition

RANKNESS, luxurious and excessive growth, hence 'insolence'

RASCAL, poor, young, lean, out-of-season deer

RAW, (i) inexperienced, uncultivated; (ii) sore or sick; (iii) uncooked

RECKONING, bill, account; 'a great reckoning in a little room', (i) an extensive bill written in a tiny space; (ii) an extravagant bill for mean or cramped entertainment. (Possible allusion to the death of the poet and playwright Christopher Marlowe, who was killed in a house in Deptford on 30 May 1593 during a dispute about a bill.) See DEAD SHEPHERD for a similar allusion. Possibly also an echo of Barabas's praise of 'Infinite riches in a little room', in Marlowe's *The Jew of Malta* (I i 37)

RECKS TO, cares about

RECOUNTMENTS, narratives of adventures

RECOVER'D, revived

RELIGIOUS, belonging to a religious order

RELISH, add a pleasing flavour to, sauce

REMAINDER BISCUIT, left-over ship's biscuit (notoriously unpalatable)

REMEMBER, 'do remember', am reminded of (V iv 26)

REMEMBER'D, 'I am remember'd', I remember

REMORSE, (i) compassion, (ii) repentance

REMOVE, go, move off

REMOVED, (i) remote (III ii 319); (ii) moved (III ii 172)

RENDER, declare, describe (to be) (IV iii 122)

REPORT, 'upon report', having been given details

RESOLVE, 'resolve the propositions of', solve the problems, answer the questions posed by

REST YOU, keep you

REVENUE, income from estates; 'younger brother's revenue', all the income a younger brother can expect by way of inheritance

REVERENCE, 'nearer to his reverence', more worthy of respect as closer to my father in blood

RIGHT, regular, typical (III ii 87); proper (III ii 109); real (IV i 96); 'right painted cloth', in the authentic manner of the moralistic pictures and inscriptions often painted on cloth as a cheap alternative to tapestry; 'by right', in the proper course of things

RIGHTEOUSLY TEMPERED, correctly blended

RING TIME, time for exchanging wedding rings, ringing bells, or performing ring dances

RIPE SISTER, (i) girl who has just reached womanhood; (ii) mature older sister (of Celia)

ROMAN CONQUEROR, 'like a Roman conqueror', with a garland on his head, like that worn by a triumphant Roman military leader, to denote victory

ROYNISH, scabby, base

RUDE, rough (III vii 179)

RUSTICALLY, (i) peasantlike; (ii) in the country

SAD, sober, serious; 'sad brow and true maid', in all seriousness and sincerity

SAFEST HASTE, as quickly as possible, to ensure safety

SAFETY OF A PURE BLUSH, no more harm than a guiltless blush

SALE-WORK, ready-made goods (inferior to specially-tailored work)

SALUTE, greet

SANS, without
SAUCE, rebuke, sting
SAW (n.), wise saying, maxim
SCAPE, escape
SCATT'RED, random
SCHOOL, university
SCRIP, 'with scrip and scrippage', with a shepherd's bag and contents, i.e. with a fairly honourable retreat. Touchstone coins this phrase by analogy with 'with bag and baggage', a phrase used to denote an army in honourable retreat, clearly undefeated as it still carries with it all its possessions
SEAL UP THY MIND, (i) make up your mind; (ii) send me your decision in a sealed letter
SEARCHING OF, probing (in medicine)
SECONDED WITH, supported by
SEE, 'though all the world could see . . .' (III v 77–8), even if all mankind could see you, none would be so deceived as he is, to think you beautiful
SEEMING, becomingly
SEIZE, take legal possession of
SEMBLANCES, mere appearance
SE'NNIGHT, week
SEQUEST'RED, cut off from its fellows
SET TERMS, proper technical style of a logician
SEVEN OF THE NINE DAYS, i.e. very nearly past marvelling at such a trivial, transient, 'nine days' wonder
SHAKE ME UP, violently abuse me
SHAME, 'I do not shame', I am not ashamed
SHEEPCOTE, hut for sheep
SHIFT, expedient, trick
SHREWD, sharp
SIMPLE, (i) honest; (ii) ordinary; (iii) foolish
SIMPLES, ingredients
SIMPLY, 'simply your having', the little you have; 'simply misused', completely disgraced
SIRRAH, term of address expressing contempt, reprimand, or assumption of authority on the part of the speaker
SKIRTS, outskirts, edge
SLANDER, disgrace
SLINK BY, move stealthily to one side
SMOOTH, agreeable on the surface
SMOTHER, very dense smoke; 'from the smoke into the smother' = 'out of the frying pan into the fire'
SO, often 'provided that'; if it (IV ii 37)
SOCIETY, company
SOFTLY, slowly

SOMETHING, (i) something; (ii) sometimes inclined (III ii 376)
SOOTH, 'in good sooth', in truth
SORTS, classes of people
SOUNDED, measured for depth
SOUTH, south wind
SOUTH SEA OF DISCOVERY, as long and as frustrating as a voyage of exploration to the South Sea
SPACE, passage of time
SPARE, frugal
SPEED, 'be thy speed', grant you swift success
SPHERES, 'We shall have shortly discord in the spheres', there would soon be such a disturbance that the system of concentric spheres, upon which, according to Pythagorean cosmology, the planets and stars revolved around the earth producing divinely harmonious music by their motion, would be thrown awry, and become discordant
SPLEEN, caprice, waywardness
SPRITE, spirit
SQUAND'RING, random
STAGGER, (i) totter, reel; (ii) hesitate
STALKING-HORSE, (i) horse used for hunting; (ii) artificial horse, behind which a hunter could shelter without disturbing his quarry
STALLING, accommodation in a barn
STAND TO IT, swear to it
STAND WITH, is consistent with
STANZO, stanza, group of lines of verse
STARTLE, be astonished
STATES, ranks, status
STAY, (i) retain (I i 16); (ii) wait for
STAY'D, retained
STEEL, the use of a blade or knife
STICKS, 'sticks me at heart', pierces my heart
STILL, always
STING, sexual lust
STIR, encite, encourage
STOMACH, (i) organ of digestion; (ii) inclination (pun)
STRAINS, tunes, melodies
STRIKES A MAN MORE DEAD, inhibits all life, action, and enthusiasm (see RECKONING)
STUDIED, carefully prepared by study, memorised
STUDY (n.), aim; (v.) apply my mind earnestly to enquiring
SUCCESSFULLY, as if he would triumph
SUCK'D, with udders drained by its young
SUDDENLY, immediately

SUFFERANCE, tacit consent

SUIT, (i) request; (ii) apparel; (pun, II vii 44)

SUITS, livery, uniform; 'out of suits with', out of favour with

SUM, total; 'giving thy sum of more To that which had too much', giving all you have to an heir who already has too much

SUNDRY CONTEMPLATION OF, the fruit of many separate ponderings upon

SUPPLIED, filled (by another)

SWAGGERER, insolent boaster

SWAM, floated

SWASHING, swaggering

SWAY, control

SWIFT AND SENTENTIOUS, quick-witted and full of judicious observations

SWORE BROTHERS, pledged to be as brothers to each other

SYNOD, assembly

TA'EN UP, made up, reconciled

TAKE THOU NO SCORN, do not be ashamed

TAKE UP, settle

TANGLE, ensnare

TAPSTER, waiter, drawer of ale at an inn

TARR'D OVER, covered with the pitch which was used in the veterinary care of sheep

TAX, criticise, accuse

TAXATION, fault-finding

TENDER DEARLY, value highly

TERM, (i) period during which law courts operate (III ii 310); (ii) 'in good terms', in stylish phrases

THAT, often 'that which'; so that (I ii 111)

THEREBY HANGS A TALE, much more could be said

THINKING, imagination only (V ii 47)

THOUGH, 'though all the world could see, None could be so abus'd in sight as he', even if all mankind could see you, none would be so deceived as he is to think you beautiful

THRICE-CROWNED QUEEN OF NIGHT, Diana, goddess of hunting, who was also Selene or Luna (the Moon) in the heavens, and Proserpina or Hecate in the underworld. She had, therefore, three roles, being goddess of hunting, of the moon, and of chastity

THRIFTY HIRE, wages I thriftily saved

THROWN, be thrown or lie thrown; 'thrown into neglect', rejected as worthless

TIME, rhythm (V iii 34)

TO, to be (V iv 128); for, i.e. 'to advertise' (Epilogue 4)

TO WIT, that is, namely

TOAD, allusion to the beliefs (i) that the toad was poisonous; (ii) that it had within its head a precious stone which had magical and medicinal powers

TOGETHER, 'a year together', continually for a whole year; 'they will together', they desire to be, and inevitably will be, married; 'sure together', bound fast; 'together is', adds up to

TOUCH'D, (i) stained, tainted; (ii) accused

TOUCH'D MY VEIN, diagnosed my mental state

TOUCHES, traits

TOWARD, impending (V iv 35)

TOY, trivial matter

TRAVERSE, with a glancing sideways blow (considered disgraceful in jousting)

TRIP, walk, lightly

TRODDEN, frequented

TROTH, 'By my troth', in truth, indeed

TROW YOU, do you know

TRULY ANYTHING, consistently inclined

TRUTH, fidelity, constancy

TRY, (i) have a wrestling match (I iii 22); (ii) judge the case (IV i 179)

TUNE, 'in a tune', (i) in time; (ii) in unison

TURK, i.e. 'heathen'

TURN, (i) adapt (II v 3); (ii) return (III i 7); 'turn him going', send him packing; 'turn'd into', brought into

TURNING THESE JESTS OUT OF SERVICE, making these jests redundant, i.e. 'to speak seriously for a moment'

UMBER, brown earth

UNBANDED, without a (coloured) hat-band

UNCOUTH, (i) unknown; (ii) wild, desolate

UNDERHAND, secret, unobtrusive

UNDONE, i.e. by not paying them

UNEXPRESSIVE, inexpressible

UNKEPT, unprovided for

UNQUESTIONABLE, (i) not-to-be-spoken-to, irritable; (ii) indifferent

UNTO, as well as (I ii 217)

UNTUNEABLE, musically disagreeable

UPON COMMAND, at your pleasure, at your will

UPON MY FASHION, similar to my own

URG'D, stated plainly and formally; 'urg'd conference', invited conversation

USE, are accustomed

USES, (i) profits; (ii) customary ways of life

VACATION, period between law terms, when courts are inactive

VELVET, with sleek coat
VENGEANCE, mischief, damage
VIDELICET, namely
VILLAIN, (i) low-born rustic; (ii) wicked scoundrel; (pun on (i) and (ii), I i 49ff); (iii) lower servant (II ii 2)
VOICE, 'in my voice', so far as I am concerned
VULGAR, common, lowly diction

WAGS, goes its way
WAINSCOT, wooden panelling
WANT, be without
WANTING, needs
WARE, (i) aware; (ii) wary, frightened; (pun, II iv 54)
WARN, (i) summon; (ii) protect
WARP, (i) bend (of wood); (ii) go astray (of a sinner); (pun on (i) and (ii), III iii 77); (iii) change to ice (II vii 187)
WARRANT, (i) assure; (ii) protect (III iii 4); 'I warrant', I guarantee, I'll be bound
WASPISH, irascible
WASTE, pass, spend (II iv 90)
WEAK, causing (or consequent upon) weakness
WEAKER VESSEL, female body (allusion to I Peter iii 7)
WEARING, wearying
WEEK, 'too late a week', too late
WELL SAID!, Well done!
WHAT THOUGH?, what of it?
WHEEL, the wheel, symbolic of the mutability and inconstancy of human life, which Lady Fortune was supposed to turn
WHEN THAT, until the time that
WHERE YOU ARE, to what you are referring

WHEREIN, in a matter in which (I ii 164); 'Wherein went he?', how was he dressed?
WHETHER THAT, whether
WHILES, while
WHOOPING, 'out of all whooping', past all that exclamations of wonder can express
WIDE-ENLARG'D, (i) in fullest measure; (ii) which otherwise would be spread severally throughout womankind
WILL, (i) desire; (ii) testament; (pun, I i 70)
WIND (v.), wend, go
WINTER'S SISTERHOOD, of the same convent to which Winter belongs
WIT, WHITHER WILT, a phrase used to silence a chatterer, i.e. 'Tongue, whither are you going, that you run so fast?'
WITHAL, with; with it (I i 119)
WOMAN OF THE WORLD, (i) married, and thus having renounced unworldly and monastic chastity; (ii) loose woman
WOO, (i) persuade (I iii 129); (ii) entreat, solicit
WORKING, aim
WORKING-DAY, everyday, ordinary
WORLDLINGS, worldly people
WORM'S MEAT, mere decayed flesh, a corpse
WOULD, 'would be', would wish to be; 'what he would', what he wishes; 'what would you?', what do you want?; 'I would not', I do not wish to, or I cannot
WRANGLING, arguing
WRATH, impetuous ardour

YOUNG, immature (I i 48)
YOUR, 'your chestnut', the chestnut we were talking about